WELCOME HOME

BOOKS BY DAVID RAVENHILL

For God's Sake, Grow Up!

The Jesus Letters

They Drank From the River

Surviving the Anointing

AVAILABLE FROM DESTINY IMAGE PUBLISHERS

WELCOME HOME

Receiving the Father's Forgiveness and Acceptance:

Based on the Parable of the Prodigal Son

David Ravenhill

DESTINY IMAGE® PUBLISHERS, INC.

P.O. Box 310, Shippensburg, PA 17257-0310

"Speaking to the Purposes of God for this Generation and for the Generations to Come."

This book and all other Destiny Image, Revival Press, Mercy Place, Fresh Bread, Destiny Image Fiction, and Treasure House books are available at Christian bookstores and distributors worldwide.

For a U.S. bookstore nearest you, call 1-800-722-6774.

For more information on foreign distributors, call 717-532-3040.

Reach us on the Internet: www.destinyimage.com.

ISBN 10: 0-7684-2719-3

ISBN 13: 978-0-7684-2719-6

For Worldwide Distribution, Printed in the U.S.A.

1 2 3 4 5 6 7 8 9 10 11 / 12 11 10 09 08

DEDICATION

This book is lovingly dedicated to my six wonderful grandchildren: Micah, Lilly, Jordan, and Noah Reninger, and Levi and Marley Purdue. My prayer for each of you is that you will never find yourself living in a far country, fallen, famished, and far from the Father. Should such tragedy befall you, remember that your Father lovingly waits and longs to hold you in his arms and say, "Welcome home."

ENDORSEMENTS

The story of the Prodigal Son has been one of my favorites over the years. This is why I was excited when David asked me to write an endorsement for his new book. His fresh insights into the parable are unique and fascinating. In *Welcome Home*, David reminds us that while the story line is about a wayward son returning home, in reality, it's more about a Father who can't get enough of His children and always wants them at home with Him. Through David's new book, the running, kissing, embracing Father is calling you to a deeper intimacy with Himself. Enjoy!

—S.J. Hill
Bible teacher and author of *Enjoying God* and *Burning Desire*

David Ravenhill is one of those lone prophetic voices crying in the wilderness while the church at large is mired in compromise. I am so thankful that God has raised up this man to call us back to the simplicity of devotion to Christ. Although this book is based on an ancient parable, it is a timely message for this hour! It will challenge you to return to your Father's unconditional love and shake free from the Pharisee spirit.

—Lee Grady
Editor, *Charisma Magazine*

TABLE OF
CONTENTS

PART ONE

WELCOME HOME

SOME time ago, my wife and I spent several days together in a beautiful, refurbished old log cabin belonging to some dear friends. The cabin was located close to the edge of a stone cliff that dropped hundreds of feet to a valley below. The view from this vantage point was spectacular; we could see down to the river as well as the countryside far beyond. We said to each other that this setting would be ideal for a Thomas Kinkade painting. The road from the cabin eventually wound its way down to the valley, where there was a small, rural town. The town was unique because it was famous for one thing; it was the home of all the unclaimed luggage lost by airlines. That's right—here in the middle of nowhere was the place where all the luggage was finally sorted and sold. After asking some locals for direction, we made our way to this rather unusual warehouse. What we discovered was a shopper's paradise. Every conceivable type of merchandise was on display for a fraction of its original price. The shelves and racks were full of items. There was jewelry, cameras, bicycles, electronics, clothing, books, housewares, and even furniture. Everything was for sale.

The name of the warehouse, Unclaimed Luggage, struck me, because it implied that the individuals were negligent and forgot to pick up their luggage. Obviously, this was not the case. The place should have been named Lost Luggage, because it was lost due to the mishandling of the luggage by the airlines, not the passengers.

One can only imagine the heartache of losing something in this way. The more valuable the lost item is, the more joy one has when one sees it recovered and restored. Losing some material item pales in comparison to losing a cherished relationship.

Welcome Home is the story of God's response to one of His children coming home. It's a story that could be titled, *Lost and Found*. In the case of the unclaimed luggage, it was lost forever. God, however, never gives up on His lost children, no matter how far or how long they may stray from home. Not a day goes by that the Father doesn't longingly and lovingly gaze, waiting patiently for some sign of His returning child. Unlike the unclaimed luggage, the Father longs to reclaim every lost child who is willing to acknowledge his need and turn his heart toward Him. This is a story about forgiveness and restoration. It is for all who find themselves overcome with disappointment, mired in sin and bondage, lost, and without hope.

I pray that as you read through this story, it will bring to life, once again, God's incredible love, mercy, and grace. It really is the greatest story ever told—*Welcome Home*.

CHAPTER I

THE WORLD'S GREATEST STORY

I F we were to evaluate this story of the Prodigal Son in secular terms, it was and still remains a "box-office hit." The last 2000 years have not diminished its appeal. Young and old alike have been caught up in its vast waves of drama and emotion. It takes us from the palace to the pigpen, from prosperity to poverty, from the father to the far country, from fellowship to famine, and from the heights of holiness to the depths of sinfulness. It is without a doubt one of the greatest stories ever told, and told by the greatest storyteller of all—the Lord Jesus Christ.

We will never know how many sermons have been preached from this story. Only eternity will reveal how many lives have been changed through its message. Archbishop Trench referred to this parable as, "The pearl and crown of all the parables."[1] Others have classified it as the greatest of all parables or "the gospel within the gospels." Although this parable is usually referred to as that of the prodigal son, we must remember the story is about two sons. The older brother's life also contains some vital lessons for us all. Finally, there is the Father without whom this story would be meaningless altogether. Some have called this the story of "The Loving Father" or "The Parable of the Father's Heart."

Throughout the centuries, artists have tried to capture the essence of this story but to little avail. It would take a major motion picture to adequately depict the numerous scenes—one snapshot is not sufficient. The great artist Rembrandt tried to capture the father embracing the Prodigal upon his return home. While his painting is indeed a masterpiece, it fails to fully portray the whole story. Writers have also attempted to address their understanding of the essential truth behind this wonderful story. Some focus on the older brother, others the wayward son, while others center on the father. There is little doubt that all these have some merit. To fully illustrate this parable would require a mural a mile long. To explain it in words would require volumes. If it were set to music, the score would require every instrument in the orchestra, from the tiny piccolo to the grand piano. It remains a masterpiece two thousand years after its first telling.

While it is impossible to tire of hearing this story, repetition carries with it a downside. Over-familiarity can render us unable to glean anything new or insightful, and so we become bogged down with a traditional interpretation. This applies not only to this familiar story, but to the rest of the Scriptures also. Like the merchant who brings from his storehouse things old as well as new, we likewise should remain open, allowing the Holy Spirit to reveal to us fresh insights and applications from His Word.

CHAPTER 2

THE SETTING

WHAT makes this parable so amazing is its universal appeal. Everyone can identify with some character or aspect of this story. All of us were raised in some type of family, regardless of our background or race. Most of us, if we are honest, can identify with one of the two sons, but before we go any further, allow me to go back to the beginning.

This is the longest parable Jesus ever told, comprising the entire chapter of 32 verses of Luke 15. Jesus told this parable in response to the Scribes and Pharisees, who stood grumbling among themselves over who Jesus was associating with. Jesus was simply expressing the very nature and character of His Father. The Book of Hebrews declares that Jesus is the exact image of God's nature and glory. We could actually say that Jesus was a perfect photocopy of His Father. In response to Philip's request, "Show us the Father," Jesus said, "He who has seen Me has seen the Father" (John 14:9).

The setting for this story took place as Jesus was teaching, and the tax collectors and sinners were gathering around to hear what He had to say. According to Joachim Jeremias,

The term 'sinners' means; (1) people who led a immoral life (e.g., adulterers, swindlers; Luke 18:11) and (2) people who followed a dishonorable occupation (i.e., one that notoriously involved dishonesty or immorality), and who were on that account deprived of civil rights, such as holding office or bearing witness in legal proceedings (e.g., custom officers, tax collectors, shepherds, donkey-drivers, peddlers, and tanners). When the Pharisees and Scribes asked why Jesus accepted such people as table companions, they were not expressing surprise but disapproval.[2]

The Jewish community had little or no regard for these two groups of people. The tax collectors were nonpracticing Jews who worked for the Romans. Keep in mind that Israel was under Roman occupation—something they despised but were powerless to do anything about. Israel, you recall, was, according to God's purpose, to be the head and not the tail, to be above and not beneath, and to lend but not to borrow (see Deut. 28:12-13). Yet, here they were under Roman domination—a sore point to say the least—and the average Israelite loathed the Romans.

Those referred to as sinners were nonreligious or nonpracticing Jews. What infuriated the Scribes and Pharisees was that Jesus not only welcomed these people, but He also sat down and ate with them. The Bible actually says He was "a friend of publicans and sinners" (Luke 7:34 KJV). Now there is a vast difference between being a friend and being friendly. We can go into almost any business and be treated in a friendly manner. Those in business know that good customer relations are important and so instruct their personnel to be friendly. Few of us, however, would consider those people our friends. Jesus was not simply friendly; He was a genuine friend of sinners. The word *receives*, used in this passage (see Luke 15:2), conveys the idea of making a beeline toward. Like steel drawn to a magnet, so Jesus had an irresistible attraction to the lost and also them to Him. Jesus was and remains the sinner's friend. That was the reason He came, "To seek and to save that which was lost" (Luke 19:10).

Jesus' actions were just too much of a religious stretch for the Pharisees. How could this man who called Himself the Son of God mingle and eat with sinners? While they did not for a moment consider Jesus to be who He claimed to be, they could not in their wildest dreams ever imagine Jehovah God befriending sinners. Now before we consider how Jesus responded to these Pharisees, we need to explore who they were and how they came into being.

Some trace their history back to the time of Ezra. The Jews had been taken captive and carried off to Babylon, while a remnant was left behind in the land. During this time, they began to intermarry with the surrounding nations while adopting their heathen ways. When Ezra heard what had happened, he was appalled and tore out his hair in anger, disappointment, and disgust. He then challenged those who had married foreign wives to separate themselves from them (see Ezra 10:9-22). It was around this period that the Pharisees began to emerge.

The word Pharisee means separated. Although this movement began with an effort to please God, it ended up being a movement that provoked God. What began in the Spirit ended in the flesh. What was birthed out of a relationship with God ended in rules, ritual, and regulations. What began with a heart of loving devotion soon became governed by a legalistic sense of duty. What started in righteousness born of the Spirit ended in self-righteousness. Passion gave way to prejudice and pride. Separation gave way to a sectarian, selfish religious system that lacked love, compassion, and mercy.

Time after time, Jesus confronted the Pharisees and warned His disciples to beware of the leaven of the Pharisees. Jesus was as irritated with them as they were with Him. He saw through their hypocrisy and repeatedly addressed their selfish motives. These were not the type of people He wanted as representatives of His Father and His Kingdom, so He constantly and lovingly sought to expose their motives and distorted values.

The Pharisees loved titles of honor like Rabbi, Teacher, or Master and demanded the people address them as such. They loved to lord it over people and force people to serve their goals and agendas. Jesus taught His disciples that true greatness is measured by a servant's spirit and demonstrated this by washing His disciples' feet—a job usually reserved for the lowest-ranking slave (see John 13:1-17). No Pharisee would think of such a thing, let alone humble himself and do it.

The Pharisees loved to pray, not because they desired fellowship with God, but rather because they craved the attention it gained them. Jesus taught His disciples to pray by going into a room, shutting the door, and praying in secret, while the Pharisees stood on the street corners to be seen by all (see Matt. 6:5-6). The Pharisees loved to memorize the Scriptures. Then they would write them out and roll them up and put them in small leather pouches called phylacteries, which they wore around their heads, similar to today's sweatband. There was fierce competition between them as to which one had the most phylacteries. The Pharisee with the most became "top gun" and gained the admiration and respect of the crowd.

According to Jesus, another major fault of the Pharisees was their love of money. Money both motivated them and mastered them. Jesus warned them that no man could serve two masters. He even went as far as to say that the way they handled the unrighteous mammon would determine how God would entrust them with His true riches (see Luke 16:10-12). Money gives us the power to achieve whatever we desire. It can be used to meet the needs of others or simply used to satisfy one's own ends. I am convinced that the Lord still uses this test of handling our finances to determine how much authority He can entrust to His servants today.

Then there was the story of the prostitute who managed to enter the house of Simon the Pharisee (see Luke 7:36-39). Bringing with her a box of very precious perfume, she not only washed the feet of Jesus but also anointed Him with it. When Simon saw what was happening, he immediately doubted that Jesus was a true prophet, reasoning to himself, "If this man were a prophet He would know who and what sort of person this woman is..." (Luke 7:39). As a Pharisee, he prided himself in never touching or associating with this type of person. How then could this man claim to be the Son of God and yet allow this woman to not only wash His feet but also repeatedly kiss them? The obvious lesson here is that Pharisees and prostitutes, like oil and water, do not mix.

Much more could be said about the Pharisees. There were various degrees and groups of Pharisees—the most radical being the Bloody Pharisees. This group, not wanting to sin in any way, would walk around with their heads down so they could avoid lusting after or coveting someone or something. The problem was that they would constantly bump into things or repeatedly fall, resulting in cuts, gouges, and bruises. Their wounds became a type of merit badge of their spirituality. Bloody Pharisees became a fitting title.

The greatest tragedy of the Pharisees was that Jesus saw through their outward veneer and into their hearts. To the crowds, they appeared as whitewashed tombs, clean and spotless, but Jesus said that on the inside they were "full of dead men's bones and all uncleanness" (Matt.

23:27). Outwardly they appeared deeply spiritual, but they were in fact spiritually dead. Jesus said they would have no heavenly reward, only the simple earthly reward of being recognized and admired by the people (see Matt. 6:2).

It was their self-righteousness that Jesus despised the most. They trusted in themselves and were proud of their own achievements. Recall the story Jesus gave of the Pharisee who went into the Temple to pray. Standing beside him was a sinner. The Pharisee looked at the sinner with disdain and informed God that he had nothing in common with a man like that. He then listed all the things he had never done, repeatedly using the pronoun *I*. The sinner, on the other hand, readily acknowledged and confessed his sin and was immediately forgiven. Jesus said the Pharisee's prayer was not even heard, let alone answered, while the sinner went down to his house justified (see Luke 18:9-14).

ENDNOTES

1. Archbishop Trench, quoted in Rev. Dr. Reg Dunlap, "The Forgiving Father" (sermon), http://sermonseeker.com/sermons/Evangelistic/The%20Forgiving%20Father (accessed 9 July 2008).

2. Joachim Jeremias, *Rediscovering the Parables* (New York: Charles Scribner's Sons, 1966).

CHAPTER 3

WRONG VALUES

RETURNING to our story of the prodigal son, we see that on this occasion, the crowd surrounding Jesus was made up of these two groups: the Pharisees on the one hand and tax collectors and sinners on the other. Jesus immediately noticed the hostility of the Pharisees toward these sinners as He saw and heard the Pharisees grumbling about His love, concern, and compassion for the sinners. Now was His chance to expose the Pharisees' hypocrisy while at the same time seeking to demonstrate the true nature of God, His Father. Jesus began by challenging their distorted and twisted values.

What were their priorities? Anything of monetary value deeply concerned them. No doubt, many of them had sheep of their own. Might I suggest that perhaps they were part of a syndicate involving the priests and temple merchants? Jews traveling to Jerusalem to celebrate at one of the feasts would need a lamb to offer as a sacrifice. It was a common practice for the officiating priests to find some fault or blemish with the sacrifice the Jews had brought with them and so reject it as unsuitable. This would force the worshiper to either return home or buy one locally. The Pharisees, along with their merchant friends, would demand a premium payment for the ones they sold. This was an extremely lucrative business for all involved. No worshiper wanted to make the long and sometimes arduous journey home to select another sacrifice and so had little if any option but to purchase another. Little wonder that Jesus turned over the tables of the moneychangers and those selling sacrifices in the Temple (see Mark 11:15). God's house of prayer had become a den of robbers. Those arriving at God's house to pray were preyed upon instead.

Jesus, addressing his remarks to the Pharisees, said, "What man among you, if he has a hundred sheep and has lost one of them, does not leave the ninety-nine in the open pasture and go after the one which is lost until he finds it?" (Luke 15:4). In using the word *until,* Jesus placed no time limit on the search. In other words, He would search no matter how long it took. The more value we place on something, the more time we will spend searching for it.

As I am writing this, we have just passed the anniversary of the disappearance of Natalie Holloway, the beautiful young college student from Alabama who went missing while on a trip to Aruba with her classmates. Her mother has repeatedly told the press that she will never give up searching for her daughter's body. For the past few years, she has devoted herself to that one goal of finding her missing daughter. Jesus applies that same determination and devotion to the Pharisees' lost sheep; *until* suggests that only when the sheep is found will the search end. The sheep had value. Time, therefore, played no part in the matter. The only thing that mattered was the recovery of the missing sheep.

Jesus is slowly but surely building His case against the Pharisees. With meticulous skill, He lays a trap that will ultimately bring them face-to-face with their false values and lack of compassion or mercy for God's real sheep standing before them.

Many have made the mistake of breaking this parable into three separate parables: the lost sheep, the lost coin, and the two sons. Such is not the case. While some may draw that interpretation from this story, it distracts from the real message that Jesus was addressing to the Pharisees. "What man among *you*," (Luke 15:4) is where the real stress should be placed. Jesus was exposing and underscoring their twisted priorities and false values.

Women were also standing there listening, so He turned to address them as well. Like the Pharisees, they too had allowed earthly riches to distort their understanding of what was really important in life. Jesus had clearly stated His reason for coming, "To seek and to save that which was lost" (Luke 19:10), not to lecture men on how to lay up for themselves temporal treasures here on earth, but rather how to invest for eternity—by seeking first His Kingdom and His righteousness.

CHAPTER 4

HOW MUCH OF A PHARISEE AM I?

BEFORE continuing any further with this story, we need to pause and allow the Holy Spirit to do His work in us. We need to keep in mind, "All Scripture is inspired by God and profitable for teaching, for reproof, for correction, for training in righteousness" (2 Tim. 3:16). The Bible was never intended to be a history book, dealing with some ancient people and culture. Rather, it is the living Word of God, ever active in revealing the thoughts and intentions of our hearts while at the same time seeking to reveal the ways of God for us to walk in.

How easily we can stand on the sidelines and criticize the Pharisees, while at the same time adopting many of their same values and ways. How we need to guard ourselves from allowing a passionate pursuit after God to turn into an external expression only. While it may impress those who look on the outward appearance, it does little to impress the One who looks upon the heart. Throughout His Word, God lays little, if any, stress on the outward appearance. Instead, He emphasizes the importance of a Christ-like character. Listen to the prophet Micah echo the heart of God, "He has shown you, O man, what is good; and what does the Lord require of you, but to do justly, to love mercy, and to walk humbly with your God?" (Mic. 6:8 NKJV).

The Pharisees knew little of that. No wonder Jesus told them, "But if you had known what this means, 'I desire compassion and not sacrifice,' you would not have condemned the innocent" (Matt. 12:7). They showed more concern and compassion for a lost sheep or a lost coin than they did for their lost brothers. Perhaps the worst illustration of this lack of compassion is seen in the story Jesus told of the Good Samaritan. Lying beaten, bloodied, bruised, and barely breathing, this man has not only been robbed of his wealth but also his life. The first two men to notice him were both religious; a priest and Levite. Neither of the two lifted as much as a finger to help him but chose rather to pass by on the other side, neglecting his cries for help (see Luke 10:30-37). According to Luke's account, Jesus told this story shortly before telling this parable. The Pharisees were so blinded by their spiritual pride that they failed to grasp that Jesus was talking about them and their kind.

Jesus spoke some of His harshest words denouncing these Pharisees, who considered themselves God's representatives. He sought to distance Himself from them, while at the same time seeking to reveal the true nature of God, His Father, to them. While we no longer recognize the sect of the Pharisees, they are nevertheless still among us. While they no longer dress in long robes and wear phylacteries around their heads, we find this religious spirit still at work in the Church today.

Take, for example, the Pharisees' love for titles such as Rabbi, Teacher, and Master. Today men crave the title of Apostle, Prophet, Intercessor, etc. The Pharisees loved the utmost seats in the synagogues. Many today refuse to minister unless they are guaranteed the front seats of an aircraft—flying first class—not to mention staying in the best hotels in the city. Some love to wear a certain style of clothing that sets them apart from others or comes across as more "high and holy." Others love to "lord" it over those under them, simply because they love the feeling of power they derive from it. All of these things tend to ultimately emphasize the external and reveal the wrong values and priorities of the heart.

Jesus warned His disciples that the hypocrisy of the Pharisees was like leaven. It takes so little, but once it begins to spread, it affects every area of life (see Matt. 16:6-12). Leaven works best in lukewarm conditions rather than in heat or cold. This certainly describes the spiritual condition of the Pharisees. The Pharisees were also lovers of money. Jesus said to them, "You are those who justify yourselves in the sight of men, but God knows your hearts; for that which is highly esteemed among men is detestable in the sight of God" (Luke 16:15).

Let me return for a moment to the false values of the Pharisees. They had more compassion and concern for a lost sheep than for their fellow men. I am convinced the Church has allowed its values to become distorted in the same way. Take, for example, the matter of abortion. We have become far more concerned and compassionate toward the unborn than we have toward the unsaved. The very thought of a tiny baby being destroyed drives us to spend millions of dollars, plus countless man-hours, doing all we can to spare the life of that innocent child, but little, if any, time is spent rescuing a lost soul from eternal damnation. I know to some this is going to come across as heartless and uncompassionate. I loathe the thought of abortion and detest those who advocate its practice. The thought of taking any life, let alone the unborn, is detestable and devilish. If, however, the end result of saving one's life is that we fail to save the soul, what have we ultimately gained?

Still others are spending all their time and energy advocating the restoration of our nation, but little, if any, time seeking to restore God's

Church and Kingdom. Jesus said, "My kingdom is not of this world" (John 18:36), and yet you would never know it based on the millions of dollars we spend in "Christian politics."

Another distorted value we have is the amount of money we spend on church buildings, gymnasiums, etc. These multimillion-dollar monuments to men have little to do with the true nature and calling of the Church. Now I am not suggesting that we sit around on beds of nails torturing our bodies, but I am suggesting that we learn to differentiate between necessity and luxury. One can only imagine how much more effective the Church would be if all the money spent on elaborate buildings was invested in missions and evangelism. Some of our Christian television show sets look more like something out of Buckingham Palace than the reality of everyday life.

Having digressed a little, let us return to our story. Jesus went on to explain that after carefully searching for the lost sheep, it is finally found. It is interesting to me that Jesus never refers to the owner of the sheep as a shepherd. I believe the reason for this is that He wanted to emphasize what motivated them: money and not necessarily compassion. He does say, however, that when the sheep is found, the owner lays it on his shoulders and immediately begins rejoicing (see Luke 15:5). As a young teen growing up in Ireland, there were sheep on our family farm. Without the aid of dogs, sheep are very difficult to handle, especially one by itself. The man with the lost sheep lays it across his shoulders to prevent the sheep from running off again. This is not to be seen as an act of compassion, but as one of necessity and expediency. Arriving home, he calls together his friends and neighbors to celebrate his success in finding his lost sheep. Keep in mind it was not his love for the lost sheep that drove him to go looking for it, but rather the monetary value it represented.

Not long ago while in the transit lounge in Japan's Norita Airport on my way to Malaysia, I looked for my digital camera. I knew I had placed it in my carry-on bag but couldn't seem to find it. Several times I went through the numerous compartments searching for it. I was becoming increasingly upset with the thought that someone must have stolen it. I tried to imagine who it was and how they could have done such a thing. The camera was almost new, a Christmas gift from my three daughters, and I hated the thought of losing it. After arriving in Malaysia, I called my wife to tell her the bad news. You can imagine my joy and surprise when she informed me that I had left it at home. It was later that evening that the Lord began to reveal how easily my values had become distorted. My concern for my camera outweighed my concern for the things of God.

We can so easily become like Esau, who sold his birthright for a bowl of chili (see Gen. 25:29-34). His immediate fleshly gratification was more important to him than his spiritual well being. How quickly we lose sight of the eternal realm and become engrossed in the natural and the satisfaction of the flesh and its desires. I believe Paul revealed one of the major keys to his life when he wrote, "While we look not at the things which are seen, but at the things which are not seen; for the things which are seen are temporal, but the things which are not seen are eternal" (2 Cor. 4:18).

What is it that causes us to call friends and neighbors together for a time of celebration? Heaven rejoices over the return of a lost sinner— do we? Unfortunately, we are like the Pharisees, who derive more satisfaction from the material realm than the spiritual. We become mesmerized with the temporal more than the eternal. The things of the world become more important to us than the things of God.

William Barclay in his exposition of this passage gives us some insight into the Pharisees mind when he writes:

The Pharisees gave to the people who do not keep the law a general classification. They call them the people of the land. There was a complete barrier between the Pharisees and the people of the land. To marry a daughter to one of them was like exposing her, bound and helpless, to a lion. The Pharisaic regulation laid it down, "When a man is one of the people of the land, entrust no money to him, take no testimony from him, trust them with no secret, do not appoint him guardian of an orphan, do not make him the custodian of charitable funds, do not accompany him on a journey." The Pharisee was forbidden to be the guest of any such man, or to have him as his guest. Hear it. He was even forbidden, so far as it was possible, to have any business dealings with him, or to buy anything from him or sell anything to him. It was the deliberate Pharisaic aim, to avoid every contact with the people of the land, the people who did not observe the petty details of the law. We will understand these parables more fully if we remember that the strict Jews said not, "There is joy in heaven over one sinner who repents" but "There is joy in heaven over one sinner who is obliterated before God." They looked sadistically forward, not to the saving but to the destruction of the sinner.[1]

While we may never go to that extreme, nevertheless, our obvious lack of interest in the lost condition of our fellow man places us in close proximity to the Pharisees. Jesus said, "He who is not with me is against me..." (Luke 11:23). If we are not actively involved with the Lord in seeking to reach the lost, then we are in direct opposition to why He came—to seek and save the lost.

ENDNOTE

1. William Barclay, *The Gospel of Luke* (Philadelphia: The Westminster Press, 2001), 206.

CHAPTER 5

THE FATHER'S TWO SONS

J ESUS continues His story by telling of a certain man who had two sons; the younger one goes to his Father and requests a share of the estate. Volumes have been written concerning this portion of the parable. I searched through dozens of books and a number of commentaries, only to discover that they all approach this parable the same way. What I intend to do is to take a fresh look at this great and timeless story. I'm convinced there are some important lessons that have previously been overlooked due to our familiarity with it. A wise teacher once said that the best way to read the Bible is to inch your way through it. One can easily read this parable through in several minutes and yet fail to grasp its numerous nuggets of truth. Meditation is when one takes the time to slowly read, ponder, and pray over what one is reading, allowing the Holy Spirit to reveal the truth to us. The psalmist prayed, "Open my eyes, that I may behold wonderful things from Your law" (Ps. 119:8).

A FATHER'S RESPONSIBILITY

First of all, it is vitally important to look at the Father Himself. There can be little doubt that Jesus was referring here to His heavenly

Father. The Bible makes it clear that the responsibility of a father is to lay up or provide for his children (see 2 Cor. 12:14). The book of Proverbs states, "A good man leaves an inheritance to his children's children" (Prov. 13:22). We know that Abraham gave all that he had to Isaac while he was still living. Job also gave his inheritance to his daughters and then proceeded to live another 140 years. Concerning the prodigal son's request, "Give me the share of the estate…" (Luke 15:12), Adam Clarke, in his commentary, writes:

> It may seem strange that such a demand should be made, and that the parent should have acceded to it, when he knew that it was to minister to his debauches that his profligate son made the demand here specified. But the matter will appear plain when it is considered that it has been an immemorial custom in the East for sons to demand and receive their portion of the inheritance during their father's lifetime.[1] [Although expositors differ on this assessment, nevertheless, many adhere to this view.]

The Father in this story is described as loving, kind, wealthy, generous, compassionate, and forgiving; everything that a father should be. Like any good father, He has planned how to best provide for His son's future, as well as His ultimate purposes. I can imagine the following scenario taking place. One afternoon, the young boy arrives home from school and is met by his Father, who tells him to saddle up the donkeys. The young boy can see that his Father is excited about something. The Father rides with the young boy to the back 40 and points down the hill to the lush valley below. He then announces that He has purchased that valley with the intention that one day his sons will have it as a part of their inheritance. He explains to them that His intention in giving them their inheritance is that they will ultimately partner with Him in His purposes. He makes them understand that what He has set aside for them is not simply to benefit them but ultimately to be used to bring honor to the family name.

As the two of them ride together, the Father shares once again His heart to see broken lives cleansed, healed, and restored. The younger son, too, wants to be involved with his Father and longs for the day when he is mature enough to be entrusted with his Father's wealth. As they approach a certain vantage point, the Father points out the stream in the valley below that will provide ample water—enough to take care of irrigating the crops as well as satisfying the cattle and other livestock He plans to invest in. The Father also informs His son that He will be purchasing more cattle, along with a flock of sheep and goats. He tells him, "I want you to begin learning to take responsibility now, because one day when you're old enough, we can be laborers together." He urges His son to listen carefully to His instructions, explaining to him over and over again that his inheritance is never to be used selfishly, but rather as a means of reaching and blessing others.

He then takes him to an area of land and suggests it would be suitable for him to build a house there some day. He explains to His son that He longs to have His children as close to Him as possible, for it is to this end that He toils and labors. As the years go by, the boys become increasingly aware of their Father's love and intentions. They see the years of toil that He has invested in so that He can provide them with the means they need to be prepared in order to assist Him in the family business. We can bring no indictment against the Father. He has exhibited everything a father should be and do. Far from being selfish, He is concerned with His sons' future calling and equipping. Like any father, He has enjoyed seeing His sons develop; He longs for the day when they will join Him and labor together with Him.

ENDNOTE

1. Adam Clarke, *Adam Clarke's Commentary On The Whole Bible* (Louisville, KY: Westminster John Knox Press, 1995).

CHAPTER 6

THE OLDER BROTHER

BEFORE we look at the younger son, we will take a moment and consider the older son. As the firstborn, he was aware that one day he would receive two-thirds of the Father's wealth, as was clearly stated in the Law (see Deut. 21:17). Regrettably, as the older son matured, he expressed little or no interest whatsoever in his Father's wealth, blessing, or purpose. He never dreamed of taking hold of it. He knew it was there and set aside for his benefit and ultimately the benefit of others, but he never sought after it. He was simply content to go on living as he had done for years—selfishly living for himself. While he enjoyed all the benefits of his Father's house, he had little time for his Father.

He was totally indifferent to his calling and his Father's provision. His complacency and apathy led to almost a total disregard for all that his Father had so lovingly and thoughtfully provided for him. He knew there was more but had no interest in anything other than himself and his own self-centered world. He never considered how this must have made his Father feel. It would be comparable to receiving an invitation to a large, sumptuous banquet, the tables loaded with every conceivable delicacy, yet not partaking of any of the food. One can sense how the host would feel, after hours of labor were invested in the preparation, to have it rejected by the one it was intended to bless.

G. Campbell Morgan, while preaching on the vine and branches, states:

> What shame, what wrong, what tragedy if a branch, if such a thing is conceivable, shall grow clusters of grapes containing the wine of the Kingdom of God, and consume them on itself for the enrichment of its own life. There can be no selfishness so devilish as the selfishness of a man who takes whatever comes to him from Christ, and fails to hand it on to other men.[1]

ENDNOTE

1. G. Morgan Campbell, *The Westminster Pulpit*, vol. III (Westwood, NJ: Flemming Revell Company), 264.

CHAPTER 7

THE YOUNGER SON

LEAVING the older brother, we now focus our attention on the younger brother. We immediately react with contempt, disdain, and perhaps even anger, for we feel we already know this young man. To use a modern expression, we have profiled him to fit into the category of a hoodlum. We picture him as stubborn, selfish, sinister, and rebellious. He is the typical strong-willed child who always demanded and got his own way. We label him as the bad apple or the black sheep of the family—the one who thinks of nobody else but himself and his own interests. In our mind's eye he has ADD, is hyperactive, and is out of control. This is the child who smokes his first cigarette at the age of 7 and is smoking pot by the age of 11. Not only is he a drug addict, but he is also a slave to pornography, sex, and violence. We imagine him dressed in gothic garb, his body covered with tattoos, his ears, eyebrows, and nose pierced and full of metal adornments.

We can better imagine him as a gang member rather than a loving son, a lone ranger bent on doing his own thing. While we don't have his name, the name Jacob or Judas seems to fit. We think of him as a scoundrel, a deceiver. One who was always scheming to be first, to be cunning, conniving, and consumed only with himself…hold it. Now, take a deep breath and stand back for a moment. Before you become judge, jury, and executioner, allow me to present an entirely different scenario.

I believe we make a wrong assumption about this young man because we know the end of the story so well and automatically conclude that he was a rebel from the beginning.

Perhaps he was more like Joseph, a "Daddy's boy." He grew up with a deep love and respect for his Father. Wherever Dad went, the younger son followed. These times of being together were the highlight of his life. Like Abraham and Isaac, the two of them were inseparable. He valued his Father's wisdom and understanding and would always ply Him with questions. He honored his Father and longed for the day when he would partner with Him in His purposes: Father and son working together. The oldest son, on the other hand, was more of a loner, spending most of his time in the fields or with his friends. Rarely, if ever, did he spend time with Dad.

As the younger son began to mature, he dreamed about his Father's blessings. His imagination began to run wild with ideas of what he could accomplish once he received his inheritance. Day after day, he dreamed of laboring with and for his Father. He knew also that without his Father's provision, he was not adequate to do or accomplish anything. There was no question in his mind that one day he would be entrusted with his portion of his Father's estate and that all his Father required of him was for him to ask for it. In the meantime, he was prepared to wait. He recalled his Father's warning, "An inheritance quickly gained at the beginning will not be blessed at the end" (Prov. 20:21 NIV).

CHAPTER 8

UNDERSTANDING THE INHERITANCE

While the inheritance was intended to be of benefit and blessing to the benefactor, it was never to take the place of the one who bestowed the blessing. God's gifts and favors are never to be a substitute for the Father Himself. What God gives to us is never to be viewed as something to be owned but as something to have stewardship over. He graciously gives to us for the purpose of becoming a partner with Him in His purposes. When God made His covenant with Abraham, promising him that he would surely become a great and mighty nation, His blessings were not simply for Abraham's sake alone, but ultimately for God's greater purpose of reaching the nations. While Abraham's descendants enjoyed their inheritance of houses, lands, vineyards, and olive trees, it was never intended purely for their satisfaction, but for the greater purpose of God—that of reaching the nations.

Consider the following passage from *The Prodigal Son* or *The Way Home* in which the author Brownlow North (1810–1875) wrote:

The younger son, we read, received his portion, the portion that falls to us; God divided to everyman severally as He will. It is true we have not all received the same portion; but unless we have been born without reason, and so not accountable beings, we have all received from God certain talents, a certain amount of power, and riches, and wisdom, and strength, by the right employment of which we can bring honor and glory and blessing to God.

And for the right employment of these talents we are accountable to God. To give us anything with which we can serve Him is a great gift, a great condescension, a great mercy; but the gift entails a responsibility. Many appear not to think so; many live as if there were no hereafter, no God, no death, no account to be rendered; but unless such repent and believe the Gospel woe to them in the day of judgment...The prodigal acted as if his father had given him his portion simply to render him independent of him, and he greatly sinned against his father; and as he sinned, so sins everyman, no matter how much better he may think himself than the prodigal, who spends his portion as seems right in his own eyes, without reference to...God the Giver.

The Psalmist hit the nail on the head when he wrote. "God be gracious to us and bless us, and cause His face to shine upon us...That Your way may be known on the earth...The earth has yielded its produce; God, our God, blesses us...that all the ends of the earth may fear Him" (Ps. 67:1-2,6-7).

No matter what type of calling or gifting God may entrust to us, we must always keep in mind that its ultimate purpose is for His glory alone.

Solomon's wisdom and Samson's strength were not given by God simply to amaze the crowds and thereby draw attention to themselves, but rather to testify to the great wisdom and power of God. John explains to us in the Book of Revelation (see Rev. 19:10) that any true prophecy is to ultimately bear testimony to Jesus, and yet how often we tend to glorify the one giving the word rather than the source Himself.

With the passing of years, this lad developed into a son any father would be proud to call his own. One thing that always bothered the younger brother was that his older brother remained so passive, indifferent, and complacent toward all that their Father was working toward. Why didn't he ask? Why didn't he show some interest in his Father's business? His Father had repeatedly told them both, "If you ask Me anything in My name, I will do it" (John 14:14), and boys, "You do not have because you do not ask" (James 4:2).

The youngest son understood his Father's heart and knew that everything his Father provided was for his good and the benefit of others. How often he recalled his Father telling him, "Eye has not seen, nor ear heard, nor have entered into the heart of man" all that I have prepared for you (see 1 Cor. 2:9). To not ask was to insult his Father and thereby trample underfoot His gracious provision and blessing. Not asking implied that what his Father had worked so hard to provide and set aside for His children was not worth asking for. For the firstborn to not ask was in many ways similar to Esau, who despised his birthright, something that deeply troubled his young brother.

The Bible repeatedly reveals God as a generous giver, "every good and perfect gift is from above" (James 1:17 NIV). When the apostle Paul was preaching on Mars Hill (see Acts 17), he portrayed God as the One who gives life to all. What a contrast to other gods, who were always demanding gifts from those who worshiped them. John tells us,

"God so loved the world, that He gave His only begotten Son" (John 3:16). James tells us that if we lack wisdom, all we have to do is ask, and God will give it to us (see James 1:5).

Throughout the Scriptures, we have numerous examples of men desiring more from God. Jacob wrestled with the Angel of the Lord and refused to give up his fight until he received the blessing he so desperately wanted (see Gen. 32:24-32). Elisha begged Elijah for a double portion of his mantle (see 2 Kings 2:9). Caleb never forgot the first time he saw the hill country in the Promised Land. Forty years later, he said to Joshua, "Give me this mountain" (Josh. 14:12 KJV). Paul pursued God with a passion, longing to know Him more. David likewise craved the presence of God as the deer pants for the water (see Ps. 42:1). Jabez cried out to God for blessing and enlargement (see 1 Chron. 4:10). We are exhorted to earnestly desire spiritual gifts (see 1 Cor. 14:1).

God's resources are available to all who ask. There are vast stores of wisdom, knowledge, understanding, and revelation that we have never tapped into. Yes, His wealth is available to all who have a genuine desire to be equipped for His pleasure and purpose. God gave to the Church men who were apostles, prophets, evangelists, pastors, and teachers for the equipping of the saints and for the work of the ministry (see Eph. 4:11-12). God always provides the resources that we need in order to accomplish His purposes. Jesus stated, "Your Father has chosen gladly to give you the kingdom" (Luke 12:32).

Why is it that we have looked so negatively on this young son's request? What's wrong with, "Father, give me"? We admire Solomon's request for wisdom (see 1 Kings 3:6-9). Thousands of messages have been preached on Jacob's insistence, "I will not let you go unless you bless me" (Gen. 32:26). Nobody interprets that desperate desire with wrongdoing, yet when it comes to the youngest son's request, we immediately react in a negative way, as though to ask was not only wrong, but also evil.

It is vitally important at this stage of the story to keep an open mind. I believe there are some essential lessons and truths we can learn if we can only set aside our own preconceived prejudice and let go of our traditional interpretation. Hopefully by now one can see where I am going. The older brother represents the old wineskin mentality and those believers who are perfectly content with the status quo. They have little desire for more of God. They are content with business as usual. Motivated mainly by selfishness, they only want to be sure that their heavenly home is secure. Apart from that, they have no real interest in spiritual things. Trying to encourage them to read their Bibles, let alone pray, is an almost impossible task. They know nothing of spending time alone with the Lord. To most of them, the cry "more Lord" has never been part of their spiritual vocabulary.

Like babes never weaned from the bottle, they have little, if any, desire to grow into spiritually mature men or women of God. Children have a tendency to live in their own world with almost total disregard for their future or concern for others. Not only is this true in the natural, but in the spiritual realm also. Spiritual babes are more than eager to receive, but reluctant to give. Their sole concern with regard to the future is simply their own security and happiness. True spiritual maturity is when we become involved in our Father's business and we're less concerned about Him being involved in ours.

Whenever something new happens that they don't understand, these older brothers denounce it and quickly put out the fire. Many of those who have had some past experience with God quickly become the persecutors of the present move or visitation. Some have also made the mistake of comparing the present to the past, as though God was incapable of doing something new. I am not suggesting that we swallow everything we see, hook, line, and sinker. That would be foolish, irresponsible, and dangerous. We need to constantly examine everything in the light of God's Word. I do believe that God has provided us with everything that pertains to life and godliness and that He never refuses those who come seeking and desiring more (see 2 Pet. 1:3).

The younger son represents a new generation of men and women (nothing to do with age) who remain dissatisfied with what they have seen and experienced. These dear saints are hungry for more of God. Like Gideon of old, they voice his cry, "O my lord, if the Lord is with us, why then has all this happened to us? And where are all His miracles which our fathers told us about?" (Judg. 6:13). They have feasted on books about revival and have devoured the writings and stories of men like John G. Lake, Smith Wigglesworth, Charles Finney, David Brainard, George Whitefield, John Wesley, William Booth, and many other great men of God who impacted their generation with the Gospel of the Kingdom. As I travel around the country, I constantly meet young men and women who express this longing for more of God. Their cry can be summed up in the popular phrase, "More Lord."

I am convinced that the younger son's journey began with a genuine cry for "more." He knew that his Father had vast resources available for the asking. This was not forbidden territory. He simply desired all that his Father had in store for him and was not content to live on the crumbs when his Father had prepared such a lavish feast. I'm reminded of the old song, which says:

Every promise in the Book is mine,
Every chapter, every verse, every line...
This is true, that "All the promises are yea and amen in

Christ."

If so, then why not ask?

Let me remind you of Paul's letter to the Romans where he expresses his longing to see them, "That I may impart some spiritual gift to you, that you may be established" (Rom. 1:11). Whatever gift Paul was desirous of imparting to them was intended for the purpose of establishing them in the things of God. Likewise, I am convinced God has resources available to each and every one of us that can be used to establish His purpose in us and through us. He does not send us forth without supplying all that we need to accomplish His purposes.

The younger brother's request, "Father, give me," was in no way offensive to his Father but rather delighted his Father immensely. This was what the Father had intended for His son's future equipping. It was his Father's good pleasure to give it to him. Considering the parable further, it is important to remember that everything the Father made available to the younger son was also available to the older brother; He divided His wealth "between them."

The younger son soon takes possession of his inheritance. The land next to the back 40 was now officially his, along with the cattle, sheep, horses, and oxen, not to mention all the lush pasture land in the valley. These were part of the inheritance his Father so lovingly and willingly prepared for him. Although he had grown up knowing and being surrounded by all of these things, they had now been entrusted to his care and stewardship. He had finally been entrusted with his Father's "blessing."

Many a son since has cried out desiring more from God in order to adequately and effectively minister under the power and anointing of the Spirit. They have sensed their lack and cried out to God for His resources to meet the needs of those around them. Recall the story Jesus

told His disciples in response to their request, "Teach us to pray...."
Jesus, after giving His disciples the Lord's Prayer, goes on to tell the
story of the man who arrived at his friend's home at midnight. His guest
is famished due to the long journey and the lateness of the hour. He has
been unable to purchase food and looks to his friend to meet his needs.
His friend and host, however, not having anything to set before him,
immediately goes to his neighbor's house and begins pounding on his
door. Even though his neighbor has already gone to bed, he gets up and
provides him with whatever he needs (see Luke 11:1-13). Jesus, in
telling this story, is emphasizing the importance of prayer. Like the host,
you and I do not have what it takes to meet the needs of those around
us. We will forever be confronted with friends who come to us at some
midnight hour in their lives looking for answers. Prayer ushers us into
the presence of God, who gladly provides us with whatever we need to
meet their need.

CHAPTER 9

NOT MANY DAYS LATER

THIS phrase brings us back to the younger brother. It is important to keep in mind that after receiving his inheritance, he does not immediately set out for the far country. His departure takes place "not many days later" (Luke 15:13). I can imagine that during those first days, he was constantly seeking his Father for advice regarding some aspect of his inheritance. After all, he was very aware of his inadequacies and weaknesses and needed his Father's wisdom and instruction. Initially, he recognized his need of dependency and thought nothing of spending hours alone with his Father, seeking for all the wisdom and understanding He had to offer. Night after night he would tell his Father of his daily activities and how the gifts He had given him were being used to meet the needs of so many. His Father would no doubt be pleased with the way His son was using his inheritance. He told his Father of the numerous healings and deliverances he had seen. Together they rejoiced in seeing lives changed and transformed, captives set free, and the brokenhearted brought back to wholeness.

Day after day, the younger son could see the look of pleasure on his Father's face as he shared with Him all the wonderful things that he was seeing accomplished through his Father's gifts. The more he saw accomplished, the more he wanted his Father's blessing. The weeks turned into months, and he became increasingly aware of all that had been accomplished through his Father's gifts. He was beginning to appreciate all that was available to him simply by asking. This, in turn, caused him to press in for more. He would often set time aside to fast and pray, longing for an increase in his level of anointing. Every spare minute was given to studying his Father's Word. During this time, he became inseparable from his Father, spending more time with his Father than in ministry. His greatest joy was to know they were laboring together. These times alone with his Father became the real joy of his life. His Father would repeatedly tell him that He was well pleased with what He saw in His son, as well as how he was bringing honor to the family name.

This was the way the Father envisioned things—He never intended for His sons to live independently from Himself. When He divided His wealth between them, it consisted of more than just material gain. It was His life. His intention was that they would come into a greater understanding of who He really was. They were to become partakers of His nature, sharing and participating with Him. The writer of Proverbs says it so well when he writes:

> *I love those who love Me; and those who diligently seek Me will find Me. Riches and honor are with Me, enduring wealth and righteousness. My fruit is better than gold, even pure gold, and My yield better than the choicest silver. I walk in the way of righteousness. . .to endow those who love Me with wealth, that I may fill their treasuries. . .I was beside Him, as a master workman; and I was daily His delight, rejoicing always before Him* (Proverbs 8:17-21,30).

This was his Father's intention—that His sons should be laborers together with Him.

Far too many men and women of God have sought for His wealth independently of the Father Himself. They have achieved some measure of gifting and anointing, only to eventually derive more satisfaction from their gifting and ministry than from the very one who gave it to them in the first place.

A.B. Simpson, the founder of the Christian Missionary Alliance, expressed it well when he wrote these lines:

Once it was the blessing
Now it is the Lord
Once it was the feeling
Now it is His Word
Once the gifts I wanted
Now the Giver own
Once I sought for healing
Now Himself alone.[1]

The younger son soon found that his anointed ministry quickly caught the attention of the masses, greatly increasing his popularity. People began to take note that this young man had a unique gifting and anointing upon his life. It was not long before his name was nationally recognized. At first he was so overwhelmed with gratitude for the way the Lord was using him that he remained unmoved by it all, continuing to walk in dependency and humility. He, more than anyone, understood that his gifts were not something he had attained by his own effort, but rather they were given to him by his Father. Some became jealous, while others gained recognition simply by being his new friend. His gifts made room for him, and he was soon being asked to share the platform with some big names. Invitations began to pour in from all quarters of the globe. What started out as a trickle soon became a rushing torrent. Crowds of people began flocking to his meetings.

"And Not Many Days Later"

Jesus' words "not many days later" seem somewhat vague and unclear and lack any specificity. Luke, who recorded this parable, uses a similar expression in writing Acts when he quotes Jesus as telling His apostles that they will be baptized with the Holy Spirit "not many days from now" (Acts 1:5). Jesus made this statement sometime during the 40 days He spent with His disciples following His resurrection. Therefore, "not many days later" could well be defined by weeks, rather than days.

With his growing popularity, the son was spending less and less time with his father. This was not something he had deliberately planned. In fact, it was just the opposite. He considered the influx of invitations a sign of genuine spiritual success. Initially he credited all the glory for his success to his Father. This all began very innocently and did not happen overnight. It wasn't a few days, but "not many days later." What began as a genuine desire on the part of the younger brother for "more" was now beginning to reveal a potential problem.

An inheritance can be both a blessing and a curse. When God gave Israel their promised inheritance, He described it as being a land "flowing with milk and honey" (Exod. 3:8). It included houses, lands, vineyards, olive trees, etc. The Father's blessing was intended to establish His people in the land in order that they might fulfill His purpose in reaching the nations. The gift of His inheritance was never to be used independently of His purposes. Along with the promised inheritance, God also gave a caveat or word of warning. The warning was that these houses and lands might cause them to forget all about the One who gave them these blessings (see Deut. 6:12). This warning proved to be true. Israel gradually drew away from God and began to mingle with the nations. They learned their ways and ended up serving their gods, while at the same time enjoying the very cities, houses, and lands that God had so generously provided for them (see Ps. 106:34-39).

Consider how many popular secular musicians and recording artists began their ministry singing in the Father's house. These God-given gifts soon caused them to drift into the world, where they wasted their gifts and talents.

It is impossible to label all these people as beginning in rebellion, pride, and selfish ambition. I am sure the vast majority began with a genuine desire for God. Not many days later, their inheritance caused them to leave the Father's house. Others attempted to reach out to the world with the Father's love, only to find the world too powerful for them. Then, slowly but certainly, they became a part of the very people they were trying to reach.

What went wrong? As I have anguished over these verses, seeking to find some answers, I have come to this very simple yet profound conclusion. *When our demands from the Father exceed our demands for the Father*, we have begun the journey into the far country. When I refer to a far country, I am not referring to distance, but desire. The older brother, even though he was in the Father's house, was living in a far country. His idea of happiness and fulfillment was to make merry with his friends, not his Father. Jesus, on one occasion, confronted the Scribes and Pharisees by saying, "This people honors me with your lips, but their heart is far away from me" (Matt. 15:8). They were standing within reach of Him, yet their hearts were distant.

It is when our desire for the gifts exceeds our desire for the Giver that we are in danger of losing everything. It is so easy for the ministry to become a substitute for the Master. Robert Murray McCheyne was said to have stated, "No amount of activity in the King's service can make up for the neglect of the King himself." As I stated earlier in the book, the Pharisees began with a sincere desire to please God. Yet, not many days later, they became a movement that provoked God.

ENDNOTE

1. A.B. Simpson, "Himself," *Biblebelievers.com*, http://www.biblebelievers. com/simpson-ab_himself.html (accessed 10 July 2008).

CHAPTER 10

THE FAR COUNTRY

THERE are multitudes of younger sons who began well yet have ended shipwrecked. This author can personally testify to numerous "younger sons" who he has watched make the transition from the Father's house to the far country. These sons began with a sincere cry for more, a cry that drove them to fasting and prayer as they called upon the Father for His promised gifts of healing, signs and wonders, words of knowledge, greater anointing, etc. Many of these people did receive a share in their Father's estate. But not many days later, they were in a far country. How easily we can go from seeking Him to seeking His hand. When the Father becomes merely a means to an end instead of the end, we begin the transition into the far country.

F.B. Meyer, in his Bible commentary, states:

Too often we desire God's gifts apart from himself. "A far country," is not far in actual distance, but in the alienation of the heart. You may be living in a pious home, and yet be in "A far country." Sin is a waste. "A far country" is always swept by famine, because our soul was made for God and cannot live on husks. Neither things nor people can really appease our awful hunger if we are away from God.[1]

No other individual in history ever received an inheritance like that of Solomon. God challenged him to ask, and ask he did. His gift of wisdom became the envy of the world. As his gift became known, his popularity began to spread. Kings and rulers from around the world sought him out, desiring to hear his wisdom and understanding in all matters. But not many days later, the king whose gift caught the attention of the world was soon caught by the world. His desire for God was now replaced with a desire for strange gods. While he was never in a far country geographically, he was in a far country relationally. His heart had grown cold toward the very One who had so graciously gifted him and given him his fame. Solomon was in fact the prodigal of the Old Testament.

So, we ask, what went wrong? Our story continues. "And not many days later," the younger son "gathered everything together" (Luke 15:13). More than one expositor states that he turned everything into cash. In other words, he liquidated his assets. The Father's gifts were turned into money. The cattle were sold, along with the sheep and goats, the equipment and tools were auctioned off, and the land was put up for sale. Gradually, over the ensuing weeks, he turned his Father's gifts into gold.

May I suggest to you that when his Father gave him these gifts, the son never realized their potential to make him rich. His intentions in desiring more were motivated solely by the thought of being a blessing to others, honoring his Father's name, and advancing his Father's Kingdom. He hungered to be so filled with the Spirit that as he ministered, he would see people brought under conviction, having their lives changed and transformed by God. He longed to have authority to set the captives free. His desire for healing was simply to see the sick healed and his Father's name glorified. His days of fasting for a word of knowledge were to reveal to those in need how much God loved them and knew all about them. His desire for the prophetic was purely to exalt the Lord Jesus Christ, while encouraging others. His cry for a greater anointing was in order to proclaim the Word of God with authority and clarity. His motivation was pure. He simply longed to see his Father's name honored and magnified. "And not many days later, the younger son gathered everything together."

ENDNOTE

1.   F.B. Meyer, *F.B. Meyer Devotional Commentary* (Carol Stream, IL: Tyndale House, 1989).

CHAPTER 11

THE PERILS OF PROSPERITY

The heart is deceitful above all things, and desperately wicked: who can know it? (Jeremiah 17:9 KJV)

SLOWLY, the son's heart was beginning to turn from that of a shepherd's to that of a hireling. Both spend their days among the sheep; one, however, is motivated by his love for the flock while the other is motivated first and foremost by whatever financial remuneration he receives from it. Gradually, he began to use his Father's blessing for his own ends. He soon found himself focusing more on his ministry than on pleasing his Father.

Prior to this, he could preach with great authority and conviction on "the law of sowing and reaping" as he warned his friends that if they sowed to the flesh, they would from the flesh reap corruption, but if they sowed to the Spirit, they would reap eternal life (see Gal. 6:8). Initially, he was motivated purely by his desire to see men develop spiritually. The thought of seeing them stagnate deeply troubled him. He longed to see them mature into spiritual giants who could assist in furthering his Father's work. While he was aware of the fact that the law of sowing and reaping applied to the material realm, he also knew that to place the emphasis on material prosperity before the prospering of their soul was indeed dangerous, and destructive to their spiritual development.

With his popularity increasing daily, he began to rub shoulders with other gifted men and women. From these he learned that the law of sowing and reaping for material gain was the message everyone wanted to hear. As time passed, he adapted his message about sowing to the flesh and Spirit. Instead, he began to concentrate on seed faith, applying the laws of sowing and reaping almost exclusively to the financial realm. While he was aware that this was a legitimate biblical principle and could be applied both to the financial realm as well as the spiritual (see 2 Cor. 9:6; Gal. 6:7), he never wanted to err by not rightly dividing his Father's Word correctly. At first, this troubled him greatly, for he vividly recalled his Father telling him, "Look at the birds of the air, that they do not sow, nor reap nor gather into barns, and yet your heavenly Father feeds them..." (Matt. 6:26).

As a child, the son had never lacked for anything, knowing full well that his Father had promised to supply all his needs. His Father had repeatedly encouraged him to seek first the Kingdom of God and that all his other needs would automatically follow (see Matt. 6:33). Yet, despite his knowledge of all this, he chose to tell his followers that they would never reap if they did not sow—that they must sow, especially into his ministry. It never dawned on him that if this principle worked for them, it would also work for him, not to mention his new "friends."

When he first received his inheritance, one of his favorite themes was faith. He shared over and over again in his meetings how he had taken his Father at His word, believing that what his Father had told him was really true and that these same promises were available to all who believed. He recalled telling the crowds that their forefathers failed to enter into their inheritance because they did not mix the word with faith. For 40 years, his own people had wandered in the wilderness on account of the ten spies who doubted God's word. They convinced their fathers that if they believed God, they would be thoroughly destroyed by the inhabitants of the land (see Num. 13:25-33).

He had seen some truly miraculous things take place when he exhorted the people to reach out in faith and believe. He had witnessed firsthand blind eyes opening and cripples throwing away their crutches and walking. He would tell his followers that no matter how much of his Father's word they heard, that unless it was mixed with faith, it would be of no profit whatsoever. He recalled the numerous times when, during his faith teachings, he could sense his Father's smile of approval. He understood that without faith it was impossible to please God (see Heb. 11:6). But that was then, not now. The days passed and his schedule increased, and he found himself spending less and less time in prayer and more and more time with his new friends. He quickly learned from them that if faith worked for the securing of miracles, it would also work for the securing of money. Once again, he found himself emphasizing money more than miracles, and in some cases, miracles for money.

Almost overnight he became linked to the new faith and prosperity movement and quickly found he was almost exclusively running in their circles. It was here that he learned a new approach to the prosperity message. It had to do with not "appearing before the Lord empty handed." The general idea behind this teaching was that if you did not give to God, He would not favor you throughout the coming year. He would get people to give by telling them that the more they gave, the more God would favor them in return. Nevertheless, he knew that this teaching was tied to the Old Testament feasts and therefore no longer applicable to

New Covenant believers, let alone able to earn them God's favor. He knew too that his friends failed to tell the people that they were to give out of the blessing God had already graciously given them. In other words, they were not to give in order to be blessed, but because they had already been blessed. Although it had been some time since he had talked to his Father, the one thing he knew was that his Father would never insist that His people pay for His favor. It was his Father's good pleasure to give it (see Luke 12:32).

George M. Lamsa's translation of the Bible from the Ancient Eastern Manuscripts gives us this rendering of verse 13: "And after a few days, his younger son gathered everything that was his share, and went into a far country, and there he wasted his wealth in extravagant living." Many a man of God has started out in ministry relying totally upon the Lord to supply and meet his needs. Material things were of little importance. His sole passion was to reach people for Christ regardless of how he had to live. Like the Apostle Paul, the younger son learned to be content in whatever state he was in (see Phil. 4:11). He had learned that his meat was to do the will of his Father. It was the satisfaction he found in doing this that gave him his joy. Gradually, however, things were beginning to change. The influence of his friends started to erode the very principles by which he had been raised.

The more time he spent with his friends, the more he noticed they all lived in luxurious homes and drove expensive cars. Many of them dressed in the finest clothes tailored exclusively for them. His heart began to crave the things of the world. The love of money gradually began to grip him. It was then that he slowly but consciously started resisting his own conscience and the gentle prompting of the Holy Spirit. Turning from the principles his Father had taught him, he chose to follow the leading of others with similar gifts and ministries.

He observed the lifestyle of his newfound friends, and his appetite for material things became stronger and stronger. With success came money and the temptation to entitlement. Soon the younger son found himself doing the very thing he had once loathed. He bought himself a mansion and the latest Mercedes Benz. It was only a matter of time before the temptation to purchase his own jet gripped him. His friends told him he could be far more effective with his time if he had his own plane. Convincing himself that his ministry was essential to his Father's business, he signed the lease, and the jet became a reality. Although he would not admit it, he did feel somewhat superior being able to fly into town in his own jet. He was now among an elite class of men who were, in the eyes of the world, a success. Little did he realize that his Father was testing him to see how he would handle success in the realm of money. He had forgotten his Father's strong yet loving exhortation, "If therefore ye have not been faithful in the unrighteous mammon, who will commit to your trust the true riches?" (Luke 16:11 KJV).

While no one is advocating poverty in place of prosperity, we need to keep in mind the purpose behind it all. In his excellent book *Prosperity with a Purpose*, author and pastor Wendell Smith writes:

One of the dangers of preaching the message of prosperity is that some people do not hear its associated words, "with a purpose." Often, people focus on the results instead of the cause. They inadvertently, and perhaps ignorantly, turn to selfish pursuits, focusing on houses and automobiles and money in the bank. People who pursue prosperity without purpose will be disillusioned. They will not find the joy which they had hoped for, or predictably, they will become sidelined with greed or covetousness.

He goes on to compare the difference between "self-centered prosperity" and "prosperity with a purpose." In order to appreciate true biblical prosperity, it is important to understand what it is not:

- Prosperity is not about money or wealth

- Prosperity is not seeking things before seeking God

- Prosperity is not measured by what one possesses

- Prosperity is not proof of one's righteousness

- Prosperity is not proof of one's level of faith

- Prosperity is not sacrificing integrity for financial gain

- Prosperity is not loving money at the expense of loving God

He elaborates further by giving the following comparison:

Self-centered Prosperity	Prosperity with a Purpose
Focused on acquiring things	Focused on using things for God's will
Manipulation of principles for selfish gain	Fulfilling the Great Commission with a passion for souls
Using money for selfish reasons	Using money to spread the gospel
Greed, covetousness, and accumulating wealth	Giving, generosity, and distributing wealth

Power to get wealth for comfort	Power to get wealth for the sake of the Covenant (see Deut. 8:18)
Imbalanced	Balanced
Bad fruit	Good fruit[1]

The anointing can so readily deceive us into thinking we are irreplaceable to God's agenda. We allow ourselves to believe that God can't get along without us. King Saul was reminded that when he was little in his own eyes God made him king (see 1 Sam. 9:21). How quickly we forget that God made us "king" and can, if necessary, replace us. F.B. Meyer, in his study on the life of Elijah, reminds us that there are times when the Father will send us to some "brook." I quote:

> "Get thee hence and turn thee eastward, and hide thyself by the brook Cherith." The man who is to take a high place before his fellows, must take a low place before his God; and there is no better manner of bringing a man down, than by dropping him suddenly out of a sphere to which he was beginning to think himself essential, teaching him that he is not necessary to God's plan; and compelling him to consider in the sequestered vale of some Cherith how mixed are his motives, and how insignificant his strength.[2]

One of the greatest preachers of all time, George Whitfield, shares the inherent dangers of popularity from his own experience.

> On Wednesday evening, Bow Church in Cheapside was exceedingly crowded. I preached my sermon on "Early Piety" and at

the request of the society's printed it for the next three succes-sive months. There was no end of the people flocking to hear the word of God... Thousands went away from the largest churches for lack of room. They gave their full attention, listen-ing like people concerned for eternity. I now preached nine times a week. The early communions were awesome. On Sunday morning, long before day, you might see streets filled with peo-ple going to church. With the lanterns in their hands, they con-versed about the things of God. Other lecture churches nearby would be filled with persons who could not come while I was preaching.... I always preached without fee.... The tide of pop-ularity began to run very high. I could no longer walk on foot as usual, but had to go in a coach from place to place to avoid the hosannas of the multitude. They grew quite extravagant in their applause. Had it not been for my compassionate Jesus, popularity would have destroyed me. I used to plead with him to take me by the hand and lead me unhurt through this fiery furnace. He heard my request and allowed me to see the vanity of all applause, except His own.[3]

I wonder how many preachers today would consider their success a fiery trial.

John Newton, the ex-slave trader and author of the ever-popular hymn "Amazing Grace," was best known for his extensive letter writing. In response to a young man's inquiry regarding entering the ministry, he writes:

If you should meet with but little opposition, or if the Lord should be pleased to make your enemies your friends, you will probably be in danger from the opposite quarter. If opposition has hurt many, popularity has wounded more.... When you see an attentive congregation hanging upon your words; when you shall hear the well-meant, but often injudicious commendations of those to who the Lord shall make you useful; when you shall find, upon an intimation of your preaching in a strange place, people thronging from all parts to hear you, how will your heart feel? It is easy for me to advise you to be humble, and for you to acknowledge the propriety of the advice; but while human nature remains in its present state, there will be almost the same connection between popularity and pride, as between fire and gunpowder: they cannot meet without an explosion, at least not unless the gunpowder is kept very damp. So unless the Lord is constantly moistening our hearts (if I may so speak) by the influence of His Spirit, popularity will soon set us in a blaze. You will hardly find a person who has been exposed to this fiery trial, without suffering loss.[4]

Along with his growing ministry, which stemmed directly from what he had received from his Father, the younger son was now beginning to feel a growing sense of accomplishment. Initially he did not equate it with pride but simply rejoiced in the fact that he was now ministering with some of the big shots. "Little brother" had now achieved fame.

His desire to please his Father was soon superseded by a desire to please his new friends. He quickly learned their ways and rapidly adopted their methods. When he had first acquired his Father's blessing, he would challenge his followers to "ask," even as he had asked. He reminded them of his Father's words, "Ask whatever you wish, and it will be done for you" (John 15:7). Initially, he taught them to ask for wisdom, insight, revelation, or the gifts of the Spirit. Sometimes he would challenge them to ask for the heathen as their inheritance or to ask the Lord of the harvest to send forth laborers into His vineyard (see Ps. 2:8; Luke 10:2). At other times, he would stress the need to press into God for all He had in store for them, reminding them of His abundant grace. Originally his ministry focused on a passionate pursuit of God. He exhorted his followers to live a life of holiness, righteousness, and godliness. He was known for his uncompromising zeal for the things of God. Evangelism, revival, and prayer were the arrows in his ministry quiver.

It is alarming to watch the increasing trend toward prosperity or self-improvement making inroads into the Church. Ministers who once taught and preached about the purpose of God have slowly edged further and further away. They have changed the focus of their message from the Father to finances, from prayer to prosperity, from holiness to happiness, from character to charisma, from sovereignty to self, and from the sensitivity of the Spirit to seeker sensitivity.

"Not many days later, he gathered everything together." Now he was quickly learning to teach people how to ask for money. After all, he taught, we are Abraham's seed and heirs of the promise. He soon found that this type of teaching went over well with the crowds. They turned out by the thousands to hear him. By now his relationship with his Father was infrequent at best. Weeks turned into months with little or no contact. He could barely remember the last time they were together, something that he once relished. Somehow in his mind, he considered that he had matured to the point of knowing how his Father would respond in a given situation; therefore, he had no need to involve Him as much. He had listened to some of his successful friends talk about being little gods. This, in his mind, gave him the needed impetus to strike out more and more on his own without having to constantly ask his Father.

With the increase of his ministry came numerous requests for his materials, tapes, videos, CDs, DVDs, books, etc. Reluctant at first to take on staff, he found he could no longer handle everything alone. What began as a sideline soon became a major portion of his ministry. The added burden of having to lease an office and pay staff, not to mention the warehouse for his materials, soon forced him into marketing his material in every meeting. He would usually begin with some apology for making his sales pitch but then would proceed to take as much time as necessary to convince his audience that what he had to offer was not an option but essential for their spiritual development.

With his growing popularity, he now felt the necessity to insist on having a contract with those inviting him to minister, guaranteeing him a stipulated amount of money as well as a required number of people in attendance. When he first began, he was content to let God supply his needs and thought nothing of going to small gatherings as well as large. Now with the added expense of fueling and maintaining his jet, not to mention his growing staff, he could only afford to accept invitations from large mega-churches. In order to further supplement his income, he began gathering the names and addresses of those attending his meetings. Each month he would mail out a newsletter explaining how his followers or covenant partners could help him in his ministry. The money began rolling in, allowing him to indulge in whatever his heart desired. This covenant partner idea was something he had watched his friends use to their advantage. Many of these practices troubled him at first, as he knew he was not being entirely honest with himself or God's people. While he knew that the teaching of covenant was a two-way street and that, in making this pledge to his followers, he could never really uphold his end of the covenant, he chose to do it regardless. Time has a way of slowly eroding our standards unless we guard them carefully and honestly.

By now the space between him and his Father was not just measured in desire, but also in distance. He found himself at the head of a major organization that was constantly requiring his time, not to mention money. Whatever free time he had was spent trying to figure out how he was going to maintain his ministry. This monkey on his back had a ferocious appetite and was constantly hungry.

Things had begun to spiral out of control, and he had no idea what to do about it. More and more time was spent in committee meetings discussing how to raise funds, and little, if any, time was spent with his Father. As the months passed, he began to realize that he no longer saw the results he once saw. Something was missing. His message was flat and lacked the spiritual punch it once had. Little did he realize that he had failed to buy oil and that his lamp was beginning to go out (see Matt. 25:1-13). Jesus referred to it as, "When he had spent everything." Many men of God are spent and have failed to take the necessary time to replenish their lamps. To be filled with the Spirit is one thing; to keep on being filled with the Spirit is another thing entirely. "Jesus appointed twelve...that they might be with him and that he might send them out to preach" (Mark 3:14 NIV). No man has the right to go out to preach without first spending time with Him. "They that wait upon the Lord...shall mount up with wings as eagles..." (Isa. 40:31 KJV). Failure to wait on the Lord results in spiritual famine.

I was just given a small booklet "The Abba Cry" by Don Lessin. Don was a very successful missionary in Mexico for over 40 years. In this booklet, containing two of his messages, he recalls the following incident:

A brother I had never seen before showed up in the church I was leading in Mexico. He had a word from the Lord for me. He began by saying, "This is a beautiful move of God here." He then waved his finger in my face and said, "Brother, I don't know you, but I have a message from the Lord for you. You give and you give and you give, but you need to get quiet because you have some receiving to do. Jesus has some important things that He wants to say to you." I received the brother's word and thanked him for speaking it. I also thanked the Lord that He had cared enough about me to bring the word to my heart. However I confess to you that I did nothing about it. I simply went about my business of being busy for the Lord. I remember the brother God sent to me, who warned me that I needed to get quiet before God. But, at the same time, I rationalized that I didn't have the time to get quiet. I thought I was too busy to hear what was going on within me. Soon, inner frustration entered into my spirit. Emptiness began to crowd its way into my heart. Lack of satisfaction in what I was doing settled over me. Why? Because as I gave myself to the "marvelous ministry" I was a part of, I was drying up inside. In the midst of it all, Jesus was no longer at the center of my being...Ministry took His place.[5]

Eventually, the pressure of ministry became too great for the younger son. He found himself jet-setting around the nation and across the world. He became drained spiritually, emotionally, and physically. Although nobody knew it, he began to take the occasional drink to relax and help him sleep. What started infrequently developed into a habit he found hard to stop. A recent injury caused him to take some pain medication, and this, along with his drinking, soon led to drug abuse. Like a man slowly bleeding to death, his busy schedule was finally beginning to take its toll. People were making so many demands on him that he was beginning to feel used—a puppet, not a prophet. His ministry had become better known for pleasing men than for pleasing the Lord. His material wealth had provided his flesh with a measure of happiness, but his spirit man was dying of starvation.

One evening, following a meeting, he returned late to his hotel room. He was lonely, tired, and emotionally drained. He did not recall all the details, but somehow he met a young lady in the hotel lobby who gave him a smile and a wink. He had to admit it felt good to have someone show him some attention, especially a younger woman. Before he knew it, she slipped her arm around his and walked with him to his room.

The next evening, the crowds gathered as usual and he went through his favorite topics of faith and prosperity. Later that month, in another city, he began to recall the events of that night with the young lady. Not being able to sleep, he got dressed and began walking the streets. It was not long before a young, attractive woman approached him, and so the pattern began—and so did the famine.

ENDNOTES

1.   Wendell Smith, *Prosperity With a Purpose* (Kirkland, WV: The City Church). This book is no longer in print.

2.   F.B. Meyer, *Elijah* (Fort Washington, PA: CLC, 1978), 21.

3.   George Whitfield, quoted in George Weakley Jr., ed., *The Nature Of Revival: John Wesley, Charles Wesley and George Whitfield* (Minneapolis, MN: Bethany House Publishers, 1987), 68.

4.   John Newton, *Select Letters Of John Newton* (London: Banner of Truth Trust, 1965), 51-52.

5. Don Lessin, "The Abba Cry" (Siloam Springs, AR: Son Gaze Publications).

CHAPTER 12

THE FAMINE

THE Chinese have a saying, "The journey of a thousand miles begins with the first step," and so likewise does the journey into the "far country." It is the little foxes that eventually destroy the vine (see Song of Sol. 2:15). An innocent glance can soon become a gaze. King David's downfall with Bathsheba began when "a traveler" (the prophet's way of describing a tempting thought) came to him. He had a choice of righteously satisfying the needs of "the traveler" by being with his wife, but chose to lie with another man's wife instead (see 2 Sam. 11-12).

According to Dr. James Dobson, there are some 1,500 ministers a month leaving the ministry. The number one reason is due to sexual immorality. These men, much like the prodigal in our story, remember when they were desirous for more of God. They had responded to His call, spent time in preparation, and then assumed the leadership of some congregation. Many of them, no doubt, used to fall on their faces and cry out for greater intimacy and authority. They can recall the sweet hour of prayer, the joy and delight of being in His presence. Only now the months and years have taken their toll. They have left their first love. What was once a fervent desire for God has now waxed cold. The voice of God has become increasingly rare; the presence of God is a distant recollection at best. Their hearts have become cold and calloused. Gripped by discouragement, they attempted to find relief through sports, sex, money, popularity, or material possessions. The words of Jesus ring true, "No man can serve two masters...ye cannot serve God and mammon" (Matt. 6:24 KJV). The riches, worries, and cares of life have taken a stranglehold, resulting in little, if any, fruitfulness. The famine begins to spread.

The Bible makes it clear there are at least two types of famine—one natural and one spiritual. The younger son was about to experience both. Famines occur when there is a lack of rain, causing the vegetation to wither and eventually die, thereby destroying any potential harvest. Spiritual famine has its similarities. The Bible speaks of a time when there will be a famine of hearing God's voice. Without this spiritual life to nourish the soul, it eventually becomes dry and unfruitful. The younger son is not only wasting away physically, but also spiritually.

CHAPTER 13

FROM POPULARITY TO PROSTITUTES

I'M convinced that most "prodigals" do not begin in rebellion but rather experience a gradual breakdown in their relationship with the Father. I can personally recount the lives of men who started out greatly anointed by the Lord and never dreamed that they would end up squandering their lives in loose living. According to a 1996 survey done by Promise Keepers, over 50 percent of those in attendance at a stadium event admitted to being involved with pornography as recently as the week prior.[1] What is the difference between the prodigal who devoured his wealth on harlots and those who visit them online?

According to my good friend Steve Gallagher of Pure Life Ministries, there are over 25 million pornographic Websites. Like flies caught in a spider's web, there are tens of thousands of pastors who are struggling to free themselves from this demonic web of enslavement. The following excerpt is taken from a recent e-mail from Pure Life Ministries:

> One by one they come to this place…. They come from every part of the country, from around the world, from every

denominational background and from every imaginable way of life. A young college student who once dreamed of becoming a teacher now obsessed with finding and meeting girls online for sex. A beloved pastor once trusted by the families of his church for spiritual guidance now in the grip of addiction to pornography. A husband with adoring children and a faithful wife now about to lose it all after seeking companionship at a local massage parlor. Each of these men represent part of a growing river of human misery and despair that is gripping the lives of men, women, and young people—tragic trophies of an enemy that desires to steal, kill, and destroy that which is most precious to God.... Despite their individual difficulties and complexities of their situation; when you really get right down to it, there is only one hope for those trapped in the terrible bondage of sexual sin...to be reconciled to God.

Consider the following. In March of 2002, Rick Warren (author of *The Purpose-Driven Life*) conducted a survey on porn use among 1,351 pastors: 54 percent of the pastors had viewed Internet pornography within the past year, and 30 percent of these within the last 30 days. Kenny Luck reported in an article on Pastors.com that, in a survey of over 500 Christian men at a men's retreat, over 90 percent admitted they were feeling disconnected from God because of lust, porn, or fantasy. It had a foothold in their lives. In March 20, 2007, at a Men's Summit in Oregon before 2,000 men, Shelley Lubben of Shelley Lubben Ministries challenged those who were struggling with pornography to stand. Thirty percent rose to their feet. She immediately challenged them the second time, with the result that some 70 percent were standing.[2] I could cite numerous reports, all confirming similar statistics. The list is endless.

With his ministry now unraveling faster than it began, the prodigal son finds himself exposed by one of his "friends." Confronted with the evidence, he runs and refuses to listen or seek counsel. The very ones he considered his friends are now distancing themselves from him. The famine begins to affect every area of his life.

How we react during a time of famine is critical to our future survival. Abraham made the mistake of traveling down into Egypt during a time of famine (see Gen. 12:10). What may have seemed a logical step had generational as well as international consequences. While in Egypt, Abraham acquired Hagar, and the world has been dealing with the fallout ever since.

Elimelech and Naomi, along with their two sons, made a decision to leave Bethlehem in Judah during a time of famine. After arriving in Moab, they saw their two sons Mahlon and Chilion marry foreign women, and eventually die. Out of the four pilgrims who left Bethlehem, only Naomi returned (see Ruth 1:1-5). She was bitter, battered, broken, and blaming God for everything. May I suggest a study on famines in the Word of God—the causes, cures, and consequences? It is a fascinating and interesting study.

The psalmist said, "He brought me up out of the pit of destruction, out of the miry clay" (Ps. 40:2). The younger brother left his father's presence and ended up at the pigpen. Sin is an equal opportunity employer and does not discriminate by race or gender. Someone said, "Sin will take you to places you never wanted to go and keep you there longer than you ever wanted to stay." King Saul began as God's anointed. He prophesied under the influence of the Spirit and was equal to the prophets of his day. Yet not many days later, we find him groveling at the foot of a witch seeking counsel from an evil spirit (see 1 Sam. 28). His testimony was, "I've played the fool, I've erred exceedingly."

Samson, likewise, struck fear in the hearts of the Philistines when, under the anointing of the Spirit, he repeatedly terrorized them. Tragically, all that ended when he cast his pearls before swine and confided in Delilah (see Judg. 16:15-21). King Uzziah was marvelously helped until he became strong. Then God forsook him (see 2 Chron. 26:16-21).

While God has never failed men, men have certainly failed God. God is forever seeking to bring back His banished ones. The ultimate message underlying this parable is one of love, acceptance, forgiveness, and restoration. Before we can appreciate God's grace, we first have to acknowledge our sin. The person who is told that his debts have been erased and forgiven, yet has no knowledge of that debt, is never going to appreciate what has been done for him.

The prodigal, having wasted his substance, is now desperate and can think of nothing other than his survival. With his reputation in ruins, he is lonely, tired, and exhausted, and with only loose change left in his pocket, he heads into a bar to buy his last drink. Sitting and sipping his drink, he meets a wealthy pig farmer who offers him some temporary work: feeding pigs. Desperate for work and in order to survive, he reluctantly offers to engage in homosexuality in exchange for work. "And he went and joined himself to a citizen of that country" (Luke 15:15 KJV). Yes, my friend, the word Jesus used is the same word the Scriptures use of a man who joins himself to a harlot. It means "to glue or adhere to" and is used to describe a man and a wife being joined together in marriage.

Now some of you may disagree with my interpretation of this passage, and you are welcome to do so. My point is this. Sin is a cruel taskmaster and will force us to do things we would never dream of doing under different circumstances. We need to keep in mind that Jesus is addressing the Scribes and Pharisees, who despised sinners. Jesus shocked them with the fact that both He and His Father loved sinners, regardless of how far they had fallen—even those who had descended into a lifestyle of homosexuality or sexual perversion. The Scriptures make it clear, "Where sin increased, grace abounded all the more" (Rom. 5:20). Nothing would enrage the Pharisees more than to hear that God loves lost sinners, even men who have given themselves over to sexual perversion of the worst kind and the feeding of swine.

ENDNOTES

1. Blazing Grace, "Statistics and Information on Pornography in the USA," www.BlazingGrace.org (accessed 10 July 2008).

2. *Ibid.*

CHAPTER 14

THE JOURNEY HOME

THE stench of the pigpen and the loss of his money, along with his craving for food, finally bring the prodigal to a place of desperation. All this, along with his intense loneliness, now brings him to his senses. For the first time in months or perhaps years, he begins to think of his Father and his Father's house. He recalls his Father's unconditional love and compassion, as well as His great mercy and kindness. He finds himself suddenly gripped with a longing to see his Father, while at the same time he becomes conscious of what he has done and what he has become. He recalls his past and present condition.

Wave after wave of emotion sweeps over him. He begins weeping uncontrollably, grieving over all that he has done. He vividly recalls his first few months after receiving his inheritance when, under the anointing of the Spirit, he saw so many lives changed and transformed. As he begins to replay in his mind these events and the depths to which he has fallen, the tears run down his cheeks, leaving behind marks as they wash away the dirt and grime from his face. What troubles him the most is the fact that he has broken his Father's heart by violating every principle his Father had ever taught him. Momentarily, he becomes afraid, thinking, "What will my Father think of me now?" The thought crosses his mind, "I've gone too far; Father would never want me back. It's too late now. I should have returned long ago."

With his mind in confusion and turmoil, he continues to weep. Suddenly, like a light shining through an opened doorway, he recalls what his Father is really like...caring, kind, merciful, compassionate, and yet righteous and holy. He knows there is only one course of action, and that is to be totally and brutally honest about his condition. "I've sinned," he says to himself. "I've sinned. O how I've sinned."

When Jesus was telling this parable, He said the younger son "came to his senses," which implies that sin is senseless (see Luke 15:17). There is no logical explanation for continuing in it. No wonder the Scriptures tell us, "The god of this world has blinded the minds of the unbelieving" (2 Cor. 4:4). The enemy deceives us into thinking that there is lasting fulfillment and satisfaction in sin and selfish pursuits. Nothing could be further from the truth. The Bible states, "There is a way which seems right to a man, but its end is the way of death" (Prov. 14:12). Sin is contrary to the way God has created us. A polygraph test proves that sin is foreign to the way God has created us. Our very body reacts negatively to anything but the truth.

Sin's season of pleasure has quickly passed for the youngest son. Reality begins to slowly unfold, and he sees the devastating results of his own selfish choices. He realizes that he has lost everything: his ministry, his testimony, but mostly his relationship with his Father. He knows there is only one way back. Perhaps he recalled the words of Hosea pleading with Israel, "Take words with you and return to the Lord" (Hosea 14:2). Or perhaps he recalled God's promise in Second Chronicles 6:36-39 when He said to His people:

When they sin against You (for there is no man who does not sin), and You are angry with them and deliver them to an enemy, so that they take them away captive to a land far off or near, if they take thought in the land where they are taken captive, and repent and make supplication to You in the land of their captivity, saying, "We have sinned, we have committed iniquity and have acted wickedly"; if they return to You with all their heart, and with all their soul in the land of their captivity, where they have been taken captive, and pray toward their land which You have given to their fathers and the city which You have chosen, and toward the house which I have built for Your name, then hear from heaven, from Your dwelling place, their prayer and supplications, and maintain their cause and forgive Your people who have sinned against You.

Or could it be that he recalled the words in Job, "There is hope for a tree, when it is cut down, that it will sprout again, and its shoots will not fail. Though its roots grow old in the ground and its stump dies in the dry soil, at the scent of water it will flourish [Lit. blossom profusely] and put forth sprigs like a plant" (Job 14:7-9). The very scent of his Father's house causes the younger son to have hope that he could once again grow into a tree of righteousness, the planting of the Lord.

The famine has brought him back to reality and back to his senses. My father used to say, "If there had been a soup kitchen at the pigpen, the prodigal may never have returned to the Father." We need to be very careful not to thwart what God is doing. Time after time God allowed Israel to go into captivity because of their sin. This was all part of His loving discipline, which would eventually bring them home. When the affliction became too great, they cried out to the Lord. Charles Spurgeon puts it this way, "Yet it was true that the Father was omnipotent. And he was secretly touching the core of this young man's heart, and dealing with him by this wondrous surgery of famine, and of want, to make him come to Himself."

With his money spent and surrounded by famine, he does not place the blame on anyone other than himself, saying, "I've sinned." So often we take on a victim's mentality, blaming everybody but ourselves and refusing to acknowledge that we alone are responsible for our condition. True repentance is to take full responsibility for our actions.

There are a number of times in the Scriptures when individuals confessed they had sinned, and yet so seldom did their confession come from their heart. Take, for example, when the prophet Samuel confronted King Saul for his disobedience to God's command to utterly destroy the Amalekites. Saul responded by saying, "I have sinned," and then went on to say, "Please honor me now before the elders of my people and before Israel" (1 Sam. 15:30). He was far more concerned with what the people thought than what God thought. Balaam, likewise, when rebuked by the angel of the Lord, said, "I have sinned," and then added, "If it is displeasing to you, I will turn back" (Num. 22:34). He acknowledged that he had sinned, yet wanted to proceed with his plan regardless. Notice his response, "If it is displeasing." Sin is always displeasing to the Lord.

The 12 spies brought back a divided report. Ten of the spies said it was impossible to go in because there were giants everywhere. This led to the whole nation of Israel grumbling and telling Moses that if they attempted to do what God told them to do, their children would be destroyed. When Moses confronted them, Israel confessed, "We have sinned," and yet they still sought to go into the land after God warned them not to go, as He would not go among them. Consequently, they were utterly defeated by the enemy (see Num. 14).

The prodigal's prayer is one of honesty and sincerity, a prayer from his heart, not just his head. "Father, I have sinned against heaven, and in your sight; I am no longer worthy to be called your son; make me as one of your hired men" (Luke 15:18-19). Could it be that when Jesus was telling this story, He deliberately chose the words of the psalmist from his penitential Psalm 51? The youngest son's prayer is remarkably similar to David's, "Against You and You only have I sinned and done what is evil in Your sight" (Ps. 51:4). Regardless of the similarity, both prayers encapsulate what God looks for from one who is truly repentant.

Much has been made regarding the phrase, "I'm no longer worthy to be called your son, make me as one of your hired servants," even though, when he came to his Father, he never said, "make me as one of your hired servants" (see Luke 15:18-20). I believe it reveals his willingness to take the form of a servant. Prior to this, he had always been in a position of having others serve him, perhaps never thinking of the needs of others, only himself. Too often we emphasize the teaching that we are King's kids, which is true. This, however, can easily lead to the assumption that taking the place of a servant is below us and not necessary, so we tend to strut rather than serve.

Jesus took the form of a servant, not simply to teach His disciples during the time of His earthly sojourn, but to ever remain one. I have always been amazed at the teaching of Jesus when He tells His disciples:

Be dressed in readiness, and keep your lamps lit. Be like men who are waiting for their master...blessed are those slaves whom the master will find on the alert when he comes; truly I say to you, that he will gird himself to serve, and have them recline at the table, and will come up and wait on them (Luke 12:35-37).

Could it be possible that at the marriage supper of the Lamb, the Lamb Himself will be the one serving, just as He did to His disciples when He washed their feet? This writer certainly believes this will be the case.

The fact that the prodigal is willing to do the most menial task reveals to us that all pride, arrogance, and loftiness has disappeared. He is no longer just thinking about himself, but how he can be a blessing by serving others. The ultimate approval from the Father will be to hear these words, "Well done, thou good and faithful servant."

There can be no genuine forgiveness of sin without first the acknowledgment of it. The prodigal understood that even though the vast majority of his sinning took place in the far country, it was ultimately done in the sight of God the Father. When Potiphar's wife tempted Joseph, his response was, "How then could I do this great evil and sin against God?" (Gen. 39:9).

I believe one of the main reasons we see so little in the way of genuine restoration these days is largely due to the fact that we see little in the way of true or genuine repentance. I have recently been corresponding with a man who once was considered the most gifted and anointed man in his field of ministry. His gifting and reputation had taken him around the world, until he was exposed for committing some horrendous acts of sin. Initially he was quite open about his sin, but within a very short period of time, his website was slick and sanitized, emphasizing only his achievements. Having known this man, I wrote him about my concerns. He became very defensive, accusing me of having a religious spirit. He then sent me a long word someone had been given about his situation. In it there is no mention of sin but rather the repeated use of the word *stumbled*. While I hold absolutely nothing against this man, I have been disappointed in his lack of openness. Sin is treated in such a matter-of-fact way, with barely any thought given to how it affects God Himself. This man had the opportunity to use his testimony of God's mighty grace and forgiveness to encourage others, but seemingly has chosen to protect his reputation instead.

When we speak of sinning against God, few seem to comprehend the pain we cause Him. In the Book of Ezekiel, God expressed through His prophet how He was being hurt by Israel's adulterous ways. In Ezekiel 6:9 we read, "Then those of you who escaped will remember Me among the nations to which they have been carried captive, how I have been hurt by their adulterous hearts which turned away from me, and by their eyes which played the harlot after their idols...." The psalmist expresses the same thought in Psalm 78:41, "Again and again they tempted God, and pained the Holy One of Israel." Isaiah writes in Isaiah 43:24, "You have burdened Me with your sins, you have wearied Me with your iniquities." The prodigal could have simply looked at the consequences of his sins, and the negative effect in his own life, regretting the choices he had made. But no, he does not mention his own circumstances, but rather, the effect it has had on his Father. "I've sinned against heaven and in your sight." In other words, he acknowledges that his sin has brought pain and disgrace to his Father and also his Father's name.

There is no greater example of genuine repentance than that which Paul gives when he writes to the Corinthian church. Paul had confronted them about how they could knowingly allow one of their members to be sexually involved with his father's wife and not do anything about it. He challenges them to purge out the leaven before it spreads like a cancer and eventually destroys the entire church (see I Cor. 5). Their response is so thorough that in his second epistle, he commends them for the way they have handled things. Notice how he describes their actions and attitude in Second Corinthians 7:11, "For behold what earnestness this very thing, this godly sorrow, has produced in you: what vindication of yourselves, what indignation, what fear, what longing, what zeal, what avenging of wrong!" Would to God the Church today could understand and express that type of godly sorrow. The Church as we know it would be a very different place. Instead, we have compromised with the world and failed to address sin as sin, seeking to be more "seeker sensitive." We are far more concerned about offending people than we are about offending the living God.

Jesus explained that the mission of the Holy Spirit is to convict of sin. If we do not preach against sin, then the Holy Spirit's hands are tied and we remain unchanged. The Church is called to be a light in the midst of darkness, but when we allow sin to go unchallenged in the Church, that light ceases to shine, and God's purpose becomes thwarted and derailed.

CHAPTER 15

THE FATHER RAN

"WHILE he was still a long way off, his father saw him...and ran" (Luke 15:20). Here we have the only time in all the Scriptures where we are told God ran. Words are inadequate to describe this moment. Here is the Almighty God, the Creator of Heaven and earth, running toward a sinner. How the Pharisees must have bristled when they heard this.

Before the Father ran, He "saw him." Jesus said it this way, "While he was a long way off, his Father saw him..." (Luke 15:20). Are we to assume that the Father just happened to be watching the road at that particular time, or was it part of the Father's daily routine? We are told that Job would rise up early in the morning and pray for his sons, lest they had sinned (see Job 1:5). If this was true of an earthly father, how much more the perfect Father? One can only assume that the Father never missed a day that he didn't look longingly for his son to return. While the younger son was experiencing the famine in the far country, the Father was experiencing his own famine at home—not a famine of food, but a famine of friendship, fellowship, and affection. Both were starving; one for food, the other for fellowship. How God grieves over those who have turned to broken cisterns in search of water yet have rejected the Father Himself, the fountain of living water (see Jer. 2:13).

We are not told what amount of time had gone by since the son had left home. I am convinced his wealth was not spent in just a matter of weeks but rather months or even years. A young man can change drastically over the course of many months and perhaps years. No doubt the famine had left its toll on his body. He was now frail, weak, and emaciated. His face, once full and flushed with the vigor and vitality of youth, was now gaunt, his brow furrowed, his hair and beard long and matted. His skin, once soft and supple, was now rough and weathered from the long hours in the blazing sun. The little clothing he had left to wear was now filthy and torn, barely sufficient to cover his bony body. His shoeless feet were blistered and bleeding from the long and tiresome journey home. Instead of his normal walk, he now limped and faltered. With every mile he journeyed, the weight of shame caused him to stoop. He frequently stopped to regain his strength, as his body was weak due to a lack of food. As he neared his home, neighbors who should have recognized him avoided him, mistaking him for some vagrant or tramp. Yet despite all of this, his Father still recognized him and ran toward him. What an amazing thought. God never forgets us, regardless of how we look or feel or how badly we may have hurt or wounded Him.

We will run rather than walk when we want to get somewhere as fast as possible. The Father could not stand to wait for His son any longer, so He set off running to welcome him home. Sermons and books have been written about chasing after God. While they have some merit, they can also leave the impression that all the effort is only on man's part. This parable tells a totally different picture of the Father—a story of desire, determination, and drive as the Father leaps and bounds toward His son. He is beaming and laughing with joy, His arms outstretched to greet him and to welcome him home.

Far too many have a picture in their minds of the Father creeping up on his son as He holds a large stick in His hand, His face reflecting

His utter contempt, anger, and disgust. He's ready to punish His son for all the pain and reproach he has brought Him. How differently Jesus paints this incredible picture of His Father. Jesus said, "His father saw him and felt compassion for him" (Luke 15:20). The word used here by Jesus denotes emotions that come from deep within. These are not some outward expressions of concern that have little, if anything, to do with how the person really feels. No! The father's compassion is real and wells up from deep within Him. His boy is finally back.

Rembrandt, in his attempt to capture this moment, fails miserably. The painting may be worth millions of dollars, but his portrayal of this moment is sadly lacking the drama and emotion. In his painting, he has the Father dressed in a popish garb of some sort, with the prodigal kneeling in front of Him. The father is seen placing His hands on the son's shoulders, as if He is administering some type of religious ritual. His countenance is somber, with no expression of joy. The entire painting has a very formal and religious air about it, showing little, if any, happiness on the part of the Father. What a far cry from reality. Rembrandt seemed more concerned with being politically correct with the Catholic Church than correctly interpreting this great and glorious picture of the Father's amazing love. If one of the Pharisees listening had dared to paint this moment, he could not have expressed his anger and false piety better than did Rembrandt.

The two seem to collide, as the son collapses into his Father's loving embrace. Desperately, he tries to explain himself, "Father I sinned against heaven and in your sight," he sobs uncontrollably. "I am no longer worthy to be called your son." That is as far as he gets. He feels his Father's arms tighten around him. One hand holds him, the other embraces his head, as his Father showers him with hugs and kisses. His Father's love and embrace are electrifying. His body, soul, and spirit are immediately revived. He hasn't felt like this in years. He does not remember how long he was held and kissed. All he knows is a weight has lifted off his shoulders as this feeling of well-being floods over him. He sobs with gratitude. He feels alive again for the first time since leaving home.

With his Father's arms still around him, he realizes that they have left the broad way and are taking the narrow way home to his Father's house. Isaiah refers to this roadway as, "The highway of holiness," a road that the unclean were not permitted to travel (see Isa. 35:8). The son glances at his torn and filthy clothing, which is still reeking from the smell of the pigpen. He wonders how his Father can stand to be near him, let alone still cling to him. But then he remembers, "Man looks at the outward appearance, but the Lord looks at the heart" (I Sam. 16:7). His Father has already heard his confession, and his cleansing is complete. Even though he may outwardly appear to be filthy, he is inwardly clean, forgiven, accepted, and loved.

Several years ago, I was sent an e-mail telling the story of a preacher who stood one morning in his pulpit. He took from his pocket a new, crisp twenty-dollar bill and held it up. Looking toward his congregation, he asked who would like to have the 20 dollars. Hands went up everywhere indicating their desire to take it. He then crumpled it into a tiny ball and asked who wanted it now. The response was the same as before. Opening the bill, he proceeded to spit on it and then to tear it. He then placed the bill on the floor and stood on it, twisting his foot and soiling the bill. Reaching down, he picked up the now torn, crumpled, dirty bill, and asked again how many wanted it. Surprisingly, numerous hands indicated their willingness to have it. The preacher then said, "Isn't it interesting that even though this bill is torn, filthy, spat upon, and crumpled, it still has not lost its value?" I have never forgotten that simple yet profound illustration of how God values sinners.

This picture of the Father repeatedly kissing his son reveals the true nature of the Father's love toward the repentant sinner. The kiss is the expression of the one who gives it. It reveals the heart of love that God has for the sinner. An old Brethren minister by the name of J.B. Stoney put it this way:

It is not the prodigal's feelings; it is the Father's feelings about the prodigal coming home. God then says, "I am a Father who will receive you when you come back to Me, and whose heart will rejoice to welcome you." There is one Man who has told us of the Father's heart. He was the only one who could, for He was the only one who knew it...the Son of God. And He was the only one who ever knew the enormity of my offence against God, the sin that put me at such a distance from God, and He bore it. I do not know the measure of my sin, and therefore I cannot pay the penalty it incurred; but that one knew it, and He paid it. He also knew even the love that is in the Father's heart, and that love He declares.[1]

The Pulpit Commentary furnishes us with this insight:

If any wandering one comes to us and says, "Will God receive me if I ask for His mercy?" we reply, "Look at that picture, and decide; it is a picture drawn by the eternal Son to indicate what the eternal Father will do when any one of his sons comes back to him from the far country of sin. Look there and you will see that it is not enough to say, in reply to your question, 'He will not refuse you' for that is immeasurably short of the truth. It is not enough to say, 'He will forgive you' for that also is short of the whole truth. That picture says, 'O children of men who are seeking a place in the heart and the home of the heavenly Father, know this, that your Father's heart is yearning over you with boundless and unquenchable affection. That He is far more anxious to enfold you in the arms of his mercy than you are to be embraced; he is not only willing, but waiting and longing, to receive you to His side, to give you back all that you have lost, to reinstate you at once to his Fatherly favor, to confer upon you all the dignity of son ship, to admit you to the full fellowship of his own family, to bestow upon you the pure abiding joy of his own happy home.'"[2]

Listen to the man who many consider to be the greatest preacher of modern time, Charles H. Spurgeon. He says:

They imagine that God is a severe being, angry and fierce, very easily moved to wrath, but not easily induced to love; they are apt to think of Him as one who sits in supreme and lofty state, either totally indifferent to the wishes of His creatures, or else determined to have His own way with them, as an arbitrary Sovereign, never listening to their desires, or compassionating their woes,...Oh that we would come to Scripture, and there look into glass which reflects His sacred image, and then receive him as he is; the all Wise, the all Just, and yet the all Gracious, and all loving Jehovah![3]

William Barclay in his book, *The Mind of St. Paul,* provides us with this wonderful illustration from the Civil War.

When the American Civil War was in progress, and when the South had rebelled against the North on the question of slavery, someone asked Lincoln: "When this war is over, and when the South has been subdued and conquered, and has come back into the Union, how are you going to treat those rebellious southerners? What are you going to do to them?" Back came Lincoln's answer: "I am going to treat them as if they had never been away."

We often think of justification as a theological and even remote conception; but the perfect picture of justification lies in the Parable of the Prodigal Son. The son had planned to come back with his confession of sin against heaven and his father; and with his request to be made a hired servant. He is never allowed to make that request. His father welcomes him back, not to the status of a servant, but to the status of a son, as if he had never been away.[4]

So many people view themselves as second-class members of the Body of Christ—forgiven, but still not fully embraced by the Father. In her book *Lord, Heal My Hurts*, Kay Arthur shares the following story:

I have a note written to me on lined paper. The side with the holes is ragged and fringed where it was hastily torn from a three-ringed notebook on January 17, 1986.

"Your teaching tonight has so freed me to believe that God has chosen me from before time to be His, knowing full well that my life would be so full of sin.

Before I was saved, I was an adulteress. I stole the man who lived next door to my parents from his wife and children, had his child out of wedlock, and finally succeeded in getting him to marry me when our child was—years old. When I came to the Lord, I was devastated to realize what pain and suffering my sin caused so many, but especially how I had grieved my Lord. God has redeemed much of the hurt done to so many, and in His miraculous ways has us to a place of loving one another, *but I still felt that He let me slip in the back door and that I never could be truly special to Him.*" [Italics mine.] So many are still living with that same feeling of unworthiness; back door Christians.[5]

I recently came across an intriguing thought while reading Gary Wiens' book, *Come to Papa*. This is what I read.

There is something implicit in the story for which I am very grateful. It is that the younger brother did not encounter the older brother before he met the Father. Had it been the other way around, I wonder what would have happened? What would have happened to the coatless, shoeless, broken, and smelly kid if the Father had not been watching, and the older brother had met him first? He would never have made it home. One of the great points of sorrow in our day is that so often when broken children desire to come back to Papa and to get healed up, they run into older brothers first. Many times, those older brothers look like us. On the night that I first preached the message that is the foundation of this chapter, I pulled onto the freeway as I was driving to the Worship Center, and there was a girl hitch hiking. I had an immediate sense that I should pick her up. I found that she was just getting off from work, and I asked her where she was headed. She said she was going to pay her bartender. She had apparently been so desperate for a drink that she had borrowed money from him. So I started talking with her and told her that I knew where she could get something good to drink. She responded with interest, so I invited her to come along to church to taste some "new wine," and to meet the Father. She responded that she had been to church and had had enough. I felt a deep grief in my spirit as I heard her response. She had never met the Father; instead, she had encountered older brothers. She had run into people who wanted to put upon her the things they have put upon themselves—that if we do the right thing long enough and faithfully enough, perhaps there will be a party when we get done.

She had experienced the cold, small, joyless atmosphere of the older brother's influence, and it had caused her to miss the Lord.[6]

This is not the case, however. It was the Father who stood longingly looking for his wayward son to return. Listen to how G.H. Lang describes what happened.

And *what* a welcome! The father's haste to meet him; the father's kiss of love; the father's acceptance of his confession without upbraiding; the disregard of the humble readiness to take a lowly office and forgo his former dignity and right; the restoration to sonship, position, dignity; filth cleansed away; rags replaced by robes and ring; squalor lost in splendor; need swallowed up in abundance, hunger stilled by the best and richest food; misery lost in gladness! To the repentant child God acts worthily of Himself by the unrestrained impulse of His heart as Father, and endows the lowly "according to His riches in glory in Christ Jesus."[7]

ENDNOTES

1. J.B. Stoney, *Ministry of J. B. Stoney* (Sussex, England: Kingston Bible Trust).

2. Joseph S. Exell and H.D.M. Spence, eds., *The Pulpit Commentary*, vol. 16, *The Gospel According to Luke* (Peabody, MA: Hendrickson Publishers, 1985), 56.

3. Charles H. Spurgeon, *The New Park Street Pulpit*, vol. 4 (Pasadena, TX: Pilgrim Publications, 1975), 90.

4. William Barclay, *The Mind of St. Paul* (New York: HarperCollins Publishers, 1983).

5. Kay Arthur, *Lord Heal My Hurts: A Devotional Study on God's Care and Deliverance* (Eugene, OR: Harvest House Publishers, 1988).

6. Gary Wiens, *Come to Papa* (Kansas City: Oasis House, 2003), 75.

7. G.H. Lang, *Pictures and Parables* (London: The Paternoster Press, 1955), 250.

CHAPTER 16

THE ROBE, RING, AND SHOES

B EFORE we explore the robe, ring, sandals, and fatted calf, consider what the great Alexander Maclaren writes concerning these gifts.

God's giving always follows His forgiving. It is not so with us. We think ourselves very magnanimous when we pardon; we seldom go on to lavish favors where we have overlooked faults. Perhaps it is right that men who have offended against men should earn restoration by acts, and should have to ride quarantine, as it were, for a time. But I question whether forgiveness is ever true which is not like God's, attended by large hearted gifts. If pardon is only the non-infliction of penalty, then it is natural that it should be considered sufficient by itself, and that the evildoer should not be rewarded for having been bad. But if pardon is the outflow of the love offered to the offender, then it can scarcely be content with simply giving the debtor his discharge, and turning him into the world penniless.

However that may be with regard to men, God's forgiveness is essentially the communication of God's love to us sinners, as if we had never sinned at all. And that being so, that love cannot stay working until it has given all that it can bestow or we can receive. God does not give by halves; and He always gives when He forgives.[1]

As they approach the house, one of the servants appears. The Father immediately calls out to bring the best robe for His son. The son can hardly believe what he is hearing. It gradually dawns on him that his Father intends for him to wear it. He quickly finds himself overcome with emotion again and silently begins to sob. He does not deserve to wear the robe, and inwardly he longs to prove to his Father that, given time, he will prove himself worthy to wear it again; but at his Father's insistence, he slips it on. How typical of all of us who try so desperately to earn the Father's approval by our own system of works or merit. Freely receiving the robe speaks of God's incredible grace, love, mercy, and kindness, while seeking to earn it ourselves puts the spotlight on our achievements and thereby robs God of the glory.

I love what several expositors reveal concerning "the best robe." They explain that the word *best* can also be translated as "first." The implication being that he was given back his former position or rank. How often when a man or woman of God has failed do we withhold the first robe? Yes, we acknowledge that God has forgiven them, but we still refuse to reinstate them to their former position or rank, forever condemning them to a secondary role, one of slavery rather than of sonship.

Where Paul challenges the Galatians with the words, "You who are spiritual, restore such a one" (Gal. 6:1). William Barclay says the word *restore* was used by fishermen for mending their nets. The obvious message is that the net, which was damaged or torn, is now repaired and fully functional again. How many times do we fail to truly restore people? Granted, we forgive, but as I have already said, we refuse to allow them to catch fish or hold some office or position within the Church. Instead of the first robe, they are given second best.

What is it about the word *forgiveness* that we don't understand? Why is it that we totally forgive some sins, yet other sins are only partially forgiven? Take, for example, the matter of divorce. In many circles, this is the unpardonable sin. I am not for a moment suggesting that we make light of divorce. Neither do I believe we have the right to withhold forgiveness from those who have truly repented. Somehow we have developed a list of forgivable and unforgivable sins. I do not believe the Bible teaches any such thing.

I constantly marvel at God's amazing grace. When Paul writes to the Corinthians, he reminds them of their former lives. In the ancient world, to call someone a Corinthian was to demean them in the most derogatory and despicable way. Ancient Corinth was the city of vice; every sin imaginable was openly flaunted and practiced there. Listen to Paul's words:

> *Do you not know that the unrighteous will not inherit the Kingdom of God? Do not be deceived; neither fornicators, nor idolaters, nor adulterers, nor effeminate, nor homosexuals, nor thieves, nor the covetous, nor drunkards, nor revilers, nor swindlers, will inherit the Kingdom of God. Such were some of you; but you were washed, but you were sanctified, but you were justified in the name of the Lord Jesus Christ, and in the Spirit of our God* (I Corinthians 6:9-11).

In Second Corinthians 11:2, Paul says, "For I am jealous for you with a godly jealousy; for I betrothed you to one husband, so that to Christ I might present you as a pure virgin." Only God's grace can cleanse and transform a person from a sexual pervert to a pure virgin.

Floyd McClung Jr., in his excellent book, *The Father Heart of God*, shares the following illustration: "When my small son comes in from the backyard covered with mud, I pick him up and wash him off with the garden hose. I reject the mud, but not the boy. Yes, we have sinned. Yes, we have broken God's heart. But we are still the center of his affection and the apple of his eye."[2]

Several years ago, I was asked to write an endorsement for a book dealing with the life of Esther. The underlying theme of the book was the impact that can be made by being in the King's presence. The author stressed the need for preparing ourselves to approach the King. In Esther's case, she spent months immersing herself in certain oils and perfumes, not to mention trying on all the clothes that she thought would please the king. Yet after numerous months of preparation, she was still so petrified to approach him that she said, "If I perish, I perish."

As I read over the manuscript, I could not help but feel that the author was misrepresenting the nature of the greater King—God Himself. King Ahasuerus is a far cry from a type of God the Father. He was a wicked, ruthless, and a godless monarch who would have gladly exterminated the Jews if Esther had not intervened. This Persian potentate struck fear in the life of Esther, even after she had spent months in preparation in order to meet him.

The only preparation the prodigal needed was a repentant heart. He knew his Father, and he knew that if his Father gave His servants "more than enough bread" (Luke 15:17) then He would not withhold His blessing from His son, but freely give him all things. The son did not have the mentality that he would have to spend a lifetime of labor for a moment of favor. In fact, the prodigal said, "How many of my father's hired men have more than enough bread, but I am dying here with hunger" (Luke 15:17). Esther, on the other hand, said, "If I do go to the King I may perish" (Esther 4:13-17). What a contrast between the two "kings."

I wrote to the author telling him that I could not write an endorsement and explaining that those of us that come from a "holiness" background never feel worthy of the Father's love or acceptance. We tend to have the mentality that our acceptance depends on our performance. Nothing could be further from the truth. Paul, in his letter to the Ephesians, says:

> *...We too all formerly lived in the lusts of our flesh, indulging the desires of the flesh and of the mind...but God, being rich in mercy, because of His great love with which He loves us...raised us up with Him, and seated us with Him...so that in the ages to come He might show the surpassing riches of His grace in kindness toward us in Christ Jesus* (Ephesians 2:3-4,6-7).

This is the real message of the Gospel: God's amazing grace toward us—*not* our own merit that earns or credits us with His love and acceptance.

Our story continues with the Father placing a ring on his son's finger. This was obviously not a wedding band or a simple item of jewelry. Rather, it was the ring that bore the Father's crest or seal. Today's equivalent would be a credit card with no spending limit. The ring, when pressed into soft wax, left the Father's seal. It was the equivalent of a signature. In other words, the youngest son was given the authority of his

Father's name. Behind that seal was the full authority of the Father's house, with all His wealth and resources. He has given us the authority to use His name. Upon our repentance, the ring is ours, regardless of how far we have come short of the glory of God in the past. One writer refers to the ring as the equivalent of being given the "power of attorney."

When researching the matter of the ring, I discovered the following statement in the *Speaker's Bible*:

Among the Romans in the time of Christ no one was allowed to wear a gold ring unless he himself, his father, and grandfather were free-born. They had what was called the jus annuli aurie. A slave wore an iron ring, and if he became a free man he could wear a silver ring; but in order to entitle him to wear a ring of gold, an expressed decree of the Senate was required. Thus, among the Romans, the wearing of a particular kind of ring was a mark that distinguished the different classes of society and separated the free man from the slave. This is the meaning of the act to the father in the parable putting a ring upon the finger of his son when he was restored. The returning prodigal was delivered from all associations with servitude, and was endowed with the bountiful freedom of a son. And that is just the significance of it for us. We can lose the baggage of our servitude; we can throw away every suggestion off it, and just wear the signs and marks of our regal sovereignty in our Father's house.[3]

Next come the shoes. Slaves never wore shoes. No wonder that the Southern slaves of the United States sang:

I got shoes, you got shoes...
All God's children got shoes.
When I get to heaven, gonna put on my shoes,
Gonna dance all over God's heaven...heaven...heaven...[4]

While they may have known only servitude, suffering, and slavery here on earth, they knew that one day their Father would provide them with shoes and they would be free to walk wherever they liked forever, liberated from the yoke of slavery.

August Van Ryn, in his book, *Meditations in Luke*, makes this interesting and insightful comment regarding shoes.

"Put shoes on his feet." You now have a *standing* before me. We often speak of the fact that Moses and others in the Old Testament were told to take the shoes off their feet, for the place they stood upon was holy ground. But I love to think that while the holiest of men in the Old Testament were told to take off their shoes, the wickedest of men in Luke 15 had shoes to put on, in the presence of the Father God. Why? Ah, because between the Old Testament and the New stands the cross of Christ. Moses could not stand before God with shod feet, because he stood there on the basis of Law, and Law can give no one a right to stand in the presence of God. But this sinful prodigal stood on the ground of divine grace alone, and so shoes were provided for him. Those shoes suited him, giving him protection and power to tread life's way, carrying the message of "the preparation of the gospel of peace."[5]

Those who have experienced the Father's forgiveness have been given authority over all the power of the enemy. They can now, "Tread on serpents and scorpions, and over all the power of the enemy, and nothing will injure you" (Luke 10:19). Paul's letter to the Ephesians states,

And you were dead in your trespasses and sins, in which you formerly walked according to the course of this world...we too all formerly lived in the lusts of our flesh...but God, being rich in mercy, because of His great love...made us alive together with Christ...and raised us up with Him, and seated us with Him in the heavenly places in Christ Jesus... (Ephesians 2:1-6).

Wow! What an amazing transformation, from rags and servitude to royalty and all its rights and privileges.

Our story does not stop here. The Father has more in store for his son. He tells his slaves, "to bring the fatted calf, kill it..." (Luke 15:23). These phrases are all pregnant with meaning. Here we have a young man who became so famished because of the famine that he longed to feed on the pods the pigs were feeding on, and now he is about to dine on the very best the Father has to offer. You recall him saying to himself while in the far country, "How many of my Father's hired men have more than enough bread" (Luke 15:17). Just the thought of bread was enough for him, but his Father is not about to feed him as a hired servant, but as a son. No wonder the psalmist wrote that He "daily loads us with benefits" (Ps. 68:19).

There is another aspect to this phrase, "bring the fatted calf and kill it," that needs to be considered. Here let me quote from G. Campbell Morgan, whose wonderful little book, *The Parable of the Father's Heart*, is based on this very parable:

While not desiring to be controversial, there are some who tell us if we introduce atonement and sacrifice into this story, it will have to be rewritten, for that does not appear here. The first answer to that objection is that, if so, the whole of the New Testament will have to be rewritten.... Yet I am not sure that we are correct in saying "There is nothing about sacrifice here."

G. Campbell Morgan relates how:

The late professor Samuel Ives Curtiss wrote a valuable book on Semitic religions, the outcome of his personal investigation in the Holy Land on the manners and customs of the people. In the course of it, he described how when a young man had been away from home in a distant land, whether as a prodigal or as a traveler, that on his return, it was a custom to offer on the threshold a sacrifice, which became the feast of welcome. That is exactly what we find here. In conversation with Dr. Curtiss, I asked him if he had ever applied that custom to the parable of the prodigal son. He said he had never thought of that relationship, but admitted that it was a most interesting thought. This makes it more valuable. Before the son can get back into his home, sacrifice was necessary, in case there had been sin. "Bring forth the fatted calf and kill it, and let us eat." This was the very language which would be understood by all Semitic people.[6]

The word *kill* that Jesus used here is the word used for bringing an animal to the temple to be offered as a sacrifice. It is the same word Paul uses when writing to the Corinthians, reminding them, "...Christ our Passover has also been sacrificed" (I Cor. 5:7). As you recall, the Passover lamb was not only killed to make atonement for sin, but also to provide a feast for God's people as they began their journey as His redeemed people.

Ellicott's Commentary states:

It is interesting to remember the impression which this part of the parable made on one of the great teachers of the Church as early as the second century. Irenaeus saw in it an illustration of what seemed to him the special characteristic of St. Luke's Gospel, viz, the stress which it lays upon the priestly aspect of our Lord's work and ministry. We note after our more modern method, (I) that in the framework of the story, the definite article points to "the calf" that has been fattened for some special feast of joy. It answers accordingly to the "feast of fat things" of Isa. 25:6—i.e., to the joy of the full fruition of the presence of God; and there is perhaps in the command to "kill it" (the word used is the technical one for slaying a sacrificial victim) a half suggestion that this was only possible through a sacrifice and death. The fatted calf thus comes to represent to us that which the Eucharistic Feast is at once a symbol, a witness, and a pledge.[7]

Only recently did I realize that, as the Father and son approached the Father's house, He called for a servant to bring forth the best robe. This was done outside the house, as the phrase implies. I believe that many sons have been granted forgiveness *outside* of their former "house" but have not yet been brought back *into* the house they left. Full restoration takes place when a son is invited back into his former house and a celebration is given in his honor.

While I can readily forgive someone, I must admit I find it far more difficult to celebrate their forgiveness, and yet not to do so is to miss the whole understanding of forgiveness. Jesus stressed in this parable the rejoicing that went on over the finding of the sheep and lost coin. Forgiveness and festivity go hand in hand. I can well understand the difficulty of welcoming "home" a wayward son and holding a celebration in his honor. It would seem as though we are rewarding him for his sin, whatever it may have been. However, if there has been true remorse and repentance, then why not?

Now comes the celebration, "Let us eat and celebrate" (Luke 15:13). For those who come from traditional church backgrounds, it is hard to imagine that the Father would be merry, let alone dance. I was raised to believe all dancing was a sin. The Father's house was always a place of formality, order, reverence, and respect. People were on their best behavior. To laugh or show any sign of emotion was considered irreverent. While there are times for meditation, contemplation, and examination, there are also times of celebration. God created man in His image, with feelings and emotions. No wonder Jesus said, "There will be more joy in heaven over one sinner who repents than over ninety-nine righteous persons who have no need of repentance" (Luke 15:7). King David danced with all his might when he brought back the presence of the Lord (the Ark) (see 2 Sam. 6:14), so here we find the Father dancing for joy over his "boy" (son).

Any doubts the son may have had about his acceptance were now banished completely. The Father does not say, "Son, I'm going to put you on probation, then in a few months or years, we will celebrate your recovery." I believe many live under that continuous cloud of condemnation, never knowing if they are yet good enough to gain the Father's approval. They believe that the Father is still so disappointed with them that He has a continual scowl on His face every time He looks at them.

How we desperately need a fresh revelation of the Father's love. God soooooo loved the world that He gave... (John 3:16). You don't have to earn or merit the Father's love or approval. (In the case of a fallen leader, I do believe that it takes time to reestablish credibility, but not forgiveness.)

John Newton, who gave us the world's most loved and best-known hymn, "Amazing Grace," begins it with "Amazing grace, how *sweet the sound*, that saved a wretch like me" (emphasis added). Could it be that the words about music and dancing coming from the Father's house upon the prodigal's return were in his mind as he wrote these words? John Newton was himself one of the vilest of men prior to discovering the amazing grace of God.

There is a divine order in God's Kingdom, and it is righteousness, peace, and joy. We never see these words in any other order, because they have a divine sequence to them. The work of righteousness is peace, so states God's Word (see James 3:18). In other words, there is no peace for the wicked. In order to obtain peace, it is first of all necessary to obtain righteousness or rightness before God. Righteousness comes as a result of our repentance and God's provision of forgiveness through the blood of His Son. Now comes the peace that the prodigal longs for—the peace of God and peace with God. This leads to experiencing His joy unspeakable and full of glory.

The Father's celebration has it all: music, dancing, and feasting. There is no lack of expense spared on the part of the Father in welcoming His son home. Lest we fall into the trap of believing that this was an exception to the rule, we need to remember exactly what Jesus said in these words; "In the same way, I tell you, there is joy in the presence of the angels of God over one sinner who repents" (Luke 15:10). Then, quoting the words of the Father, he says, "…we had to celebrate and rejoice" (Luke 15:32).

As the music and dancing fills the Father's house, the older brother hears it as he returns from the fields. This is not some soft, sentimental background music, but music loud enough to be heard from a distance. One can only imagine the volume of noise Heaven can produce upon the return of a sinner.

ENDNOTES

1. Alexander Maclaren, *Expositions Of Holy Scripture* (Grand Rapids, MI: Baker Book House, 1978).

2. Floyd McClung Jr., *The Father Heart of God* (Eugene, OR: Harvest House Publishers, 1985).

3. Edward Hastings and James Hastings, eds., *The Speaker's Bible*, vol. 10, *The Gospel According to St. Luke III* (Grand Rapids, MI: Baker Book House, 1963), 45.

4. Jonny Cash, "I Got Shoes," *Hymns From the Heart* (1962).

5. August Van Ryn, *Meditations in Luke* (New York: Loizeaux Brothers, 1953), 138.

6. See Part 2 of this book for the full text of G. Campbell Morgan's *The Parable of the Father's Heart.*

7. Charles John Ellicott, ed., *Ellicott's Commentary On The Whole Bible*, vol. III (Grand Rapids, MI: Zondervan, 1981), 317.

CHAPTER 17

THE OLDER
BROTHER

THIS book would not be complete without revisiting the older brother. Although we have had a tendency to focus on the younger son and his sinful ways, we have failed to see that the older brother was Jesus' way of holding a mirror in front of the Pharisees to reveal how He saw them and how they needed to see themselves. They epitomized the older brother as they bristled with contempt at the way Jesus was receiving sinners and eating with them. No wonder Jesus told of the Father not only welcoming His son home, but also killing the fatted calf and preparing a special meal in honor of his return.

G.H. Lang puts it this way:

> This disagreeable person(s) is really a main feature of the parable. Here the scribes and Pharisees are made to see themselves....The younger son had acted with open abandoned wickedness; tax gatherers and sinners were notoriously evil; but these religious leaders had maintained correct behavior; they never transgressed a commandment, but prided themselves on

punctilious observance of God's requirements. The former had gone into a far country of self indulgence, with neglect of the priorities of life and religion as required by the law. These stayed at home and were diligent supporters of the house of God....The deep moral estrangement from the father came to light in their opposed attitude to the prodigal...brotherly love, sympathy with joy of their father, failed utterly. He could not and would not forgive and forget.... O thou proud, self-righteous Pharisee, surely thou art the more detestable of the two![1]

For those who have never experienced the depths of depravity, there is a tendency to pride ourselves in our own self-righteousness and look down upon those who have fallen further than we have. This, in turn, leads to a lack of compassion and then judgmentalism, believing that somehow we are responsible for our own salvation.

William Barclay writes in *The Daily Study Bible Series*:

But that is not the end of the story. There enters the older brother who was actually sorry that his brother had come home. The elder brother stands for the self righteous Pharisees who would rather have seen a sinner destroyed than saved. Certain things stand out about the elder brother.

(1) His whole attitude shows that his years of obedience to his father had been years of grim duty and not loving service.

(2) His whole attitude is one of utter lack of sympathy. He refers to his brother, not as *my brother* but as *your son.* He was the kind of self-righteous character who would cheerfully have kicked a man farther into the gutter when he was already down.

(3) He had a peculiarly nasty mind. There is no mention of harlots until he mentions them. He no doubt suspected and accused his brother of the sins he himself would have liked to commit.

Once again we have the same amazing truth here, that it is easier to confess to God than it is to many a man; that God is more merciful in His judgments than many an orthodox man is; and that God can forgive when men refuse to forgive. In face of a love like that we cannot be other than lost in wonder, love and praise.[2]

The great lesson to be learned here is how deceitful our hearts can become if we fail to remain thankful for all that God has done in our lives. We need to constantly recall "the pit from which you were dug" (Isa. 51:1 NKJV). I'm reminded again of what Peter wrote in his second Epistle, "For he who lacks these qualities is blind or short-sighted, having forgotten his purification from his former sins" (2 Pet.1:9). How soon we forget, "All we like sheep have gone astray..." (Isa. 53:6 NKJV). It would do us all good to remember that the only flock God has is made up entirely of sheep who were formerly lost and have been found.

ENDNOTES

1.   G.H. Lang, *Pictures and Parables* (London: The Paternoster Press, 1955), 251.

2.   William Barclay, *The Gospel Of Luke* (Philadelphia: The Westminster Press, 1956), 213.

CHAPTER 18

THE THIRD SON

THIS wonderful story of love, acceptance, and forgiveness would not be complete without looking at the third son. I can already hear the response of some, "What third son?" The third son is the one telling the story: Jesus Himself. We could best describe the three sons this way.

(1) The Proud Son—The older brother who represented the Pharisees.

(2) The Prodigal Son—The younger brother.

(3) The Perfect Son or Pattern Son—The Lord Jesus Christ.

No one knew the heart of the Father better than the Lord Jesus Christ. He came to reveal to mankind the very nature and character of God. Everything that Jesus did was a perfect reflection of His Father. When He wept over the city of Jerusalem, when He held little children so gently in His arms, when He raised the dead and cleansed the lepers or forgave the woman caught in adultery, He was expressing His Father's heart. Jesus never initiated anything, but simply did and said whatever the Father told Him to do and say (see John 12:49).

Who better, then, to tell this story than Jesus? The father in the story was His Father. The sons represent every son of Adam who, due to sin, has fallen and come short of the Father's glory. It does not matter whether you are the proud older brother, convinced that you have never sinned and trusting in your own self-righteousness, or the prodigal who went to the very depths of sin; both are dressed in filthy rags—one outwardly, the other inwardly. Both are in need of the Savior. The Father will run toward you when He sees *you* heading His way, saying, "Father, I've sinned." The robe, the ring, the shoes, and the feast are all waiting; but greater yet, the Father himself is waiting.

Welcome home.

PART TWO

THE PARABLE OF THE

FATHER'S HEART

THE PARABLE OF
THE FATHER'S HEART BY

DR. G. CAMPBELL MORGAN

HENRY E. WALTER, LTD.

107 FLEET STREET LUDGATE CIRCUS

LONDON E.C.4

First Published 1947

Published by Henry E. Walter, Ltd.,

107 Fleet Street London, E.C. 4,

and Printed by the Church Army Press

Cowley, Oxford

CONTENTS

FOREWORD

OUR Lord uttered the supreme parable of His teaching in revelation of the attitude of God to man in his lost condition. The three phases of the Parable constitute a wonderful unveiling of the Divine heart. In each, the greatest joy is shown to be that of God, for the deepest rejoicing was that of the shepherd who owned the sheep, the woman who lost the coin, and the father who mourned his son.

In the first, we have the aspect of grace as revealed in the work of the Son Who came to seek and save the lost. There was no effort on the part of the sheep to return.

In the second, we have the aspect of grace as revealed in the work of the Spirit, expressed through the ministry of the Church. She seeks, amid the darkness and desolation, for the lost. Here again, God is revealed patiently seeking the lost, when there is no desire on his part to return.

The third reveals the aspect of grace as revealed in the love of the Father. A love that was always set upon the sinner shone out in its brightest glory in the welcome given, so overwhelming in its tenderness and riches. In this phase, the element of will in the life of the sinner is introduced. The perversion of will took him away from home to the far country. It was necessary that there should be a return of the will to allegiance, and this expressed itself in his repentance and return. The Divine Love is the theme of the whole discourse, so full of matchless beauty. Love goes to the wilderness, continues to seek, and welcomes home.

CHAPTER I

THE FAR COUNTRY

A certain man had two sons: and the younger of them said to his father, Father, give me the portion of thy substance that falleth to me. And he divided unto them his living. And not many days after the younger son gathered all together, and took his journey into a far country (Luke 15:11-13a).

THIS fifteenth chapter of Luke is a page peculiar to him, and contains the answer of Jesus to a criticism of the Pharisees and scribes. It opens with the declaration that "All the publicans and sinners were drawing near unto Him for to hear Him," and that "the Pharisees and the scribes murmured, saying, 'This Man receiveth sinners, and eateth with them.'" One of the things that the religious rulers of His time could not understand, and did not attempt to do so, was the fact that He received and sat down to eat with sinning men, in a ordinary way. In answer to the moral teachers of His own day, Jesus uttered the words of this entire chapter.

This answer of Jesus consists of one parable, not three. We generally say three parables, and there is a sense in which that is quite permissible; the man with the lost sheep, the woman and the lost piece of silver, and the prodigal son. All such description is correct if we remember that this is one set address, continuous, consecutive, and complete. It is, therefore, really one parable with three facets. The inclusive truth is taught in the parable with three facets. The inclusive truth taught in the parable is that of the place of lost things in the economy of God; a lost sheep, a lost piece of silver, and the lost son. He showed in the entire parable how God acts in the presence of lost things. None of them is abandoned. All of them are valuable, and all of them are sought; and the way of the finding of all is revealed. This is the supreme value of the whole teaching. It shows us God's way of finding His lost things.

In the first phase of the parable, the work of the Son is the supreme subject; the Shepherd Who seeks and finds His sheep. In the second, the work of the Spirit is suggested by the woman who constantly sweeps the house until the lost silver is found. In the final phase of the parable, the work of the Father is revealed. So in that answer of Jesus, in simplest language, which every child can understand, He set forth the fact of the Divine activity in the mystery of the threefold Personality in unity, in the presence of lost things.

I do not propose to ignore wholly the first two phases of the parable, dealing in the fifth study with the shepherd work of Christ; the activity of the Church by the Spirit, and the inter-relation of the three. We will begin, however, where Jesus ended, for these are the fundamental things. We speak of this as the parable of the prodigal. In certain senses it may be true, but I think it is an unfortunate one. The root meaning of the word prodigal is one *driven forth*. That does not apply here, for this boy was not driven out. He went out. Or take the acquired meaning. We talk about a prodigal today, and we mean one who is lavish or extravagant in expenditure, and one given over to the more vulgar forms of sin. We have no proof that this young man was guilty of any of these things. I know he spent all in riotous living, but there is no proof that he was degraded. Indeed, I could argue that there was, in the very days of his darkness and misery, something fine about him. This man never lost his honour. "He would fain have been filled with the husks that the swine did eat; and no man gave unto him." He did not steal. There is a touch of fine morality in that. We have not reached the point of the parable if we are seeing the power of God to deal with the "down-and-out." I love that slogan of the Salvation Army. "A man may be down, but he is never out." That is a great thing to remember as we go to seek and save the lost. But if we simply look here for a picture of such a man as vulgarized, and down-and-out, it is not here. I would also remind you that the word prodigal does not occur in the text. The Scripture speaks of him as "the younger son."

By referring to this as the parable of the prodigal son, we lay emphasis upon the wrong point, the wrong word, at the wrong place. The true emphasis is not upon the boy, but upon his father. It is an unveiling of the heart of God, and in all that it is intended to teach, there is no more remarkable or beautiful passage in the Scripture of truth. It is a revelation of the relation of man to God; of the true meaning and issue of man's separation from God; and supremely of the infinite grace and tenderness of the Father's heart.

In this meditation on the first phase of the story, we see first the revealed relationship between man and God. "A certain man had two sons." Secondly, the way in which man has lost that relation, the way of separation, is revealed in the opening sentences, "Father, give me the portion of substance that falleth to me. And he divided unto them his living. And not many days after the younger son gathered all together, and took his journey." Finally to where it leads, "the far country."

What is the relationship existing? "A certain man had two sons." Here we are brought face to face with the underlying fact of human life. The relationship between God and man is that man is a son of God.

One is always conscious of the acute theologian who enjoys seeing if the preacher is orthodox. I am content to abide by the Book, and the revelation of the Book, and the truth as revealed in the Book. It may be argued Jesus said of the Jews, "Ye are of your father the devil." He certainly did, but how did they become children of the devil? Not by creation. The fundamental fact revealed here is that whatever is said about this younger son, he was the son of his father. That is the whole testimony of the Bible concerning human life. The story in Genesis sets the whole creation in relation to God. All creation depended upon God's wisdom and power and fiat. In that ancient story of poetic suggestiveness and truth, we see before man appeared upon the created scene, there was counsel. "Let Us make man in Our image, after Our likeness." It was by the Divine breath man became a living soul.

If in the ancient story we are immediately introduced to the fact of sin; and if through all the records of the past we find references to sin and death, it is nevertheless impossible to escape from the fact that man is a distinct creation of God. Everything essential to his being is divine in its origin. Such is the conception of the whole of the Old Testament. On that day in the dark period in the history of God's ancient people, when they had coined a false proverb and were bandying it about as a cloak for their own wrong-doing, blaming their fathers for their sin, they said, "The fathers have eaten sour grapes, and the children's teeth are set on edge." That is untrue. It is a lie, often quoted today. It was dealt with very fully by the prophet Ezekiel. In answer to that false proverb, he said, "This is the truth, 'All souls are Mine; as the soul of the father, so also the soul of the son is Mine; the soul that sinneth, it shall die.'" No man shall die for his father's sin. There is first-hand relationship between man and God.

Turning to the New Testament, we take one illustration from the Gospel stories. The Gospel of Luke is peculiarly the Gospel of the humanity of our Lord, and the Gospel for humanity generally. Matthew was written for the Jew; Mark, perchance, for the Roman citizen; and John for the mystic and the believer. It is a significant fact that when Luke would tell the story of the Logos of Jesus—for that is what he called Him at the commencement of his writing—when dealing with His human nature, he inserted a genealogy, not that of the adoption of Jesus by Joseph, but that of the actual birth of Jesus through the line of Mary. Luke went back, sweeping through Abraham until he came to Adam, the first man. How did he end? "Adam, who was the son of God." There is a sense in which that applies to all the names in the long list of that genealogy, and of all men everywhere.

Paul, preaching on Mars Hill, quoted from the Greek poets, and verified the accuracy of their declaration, "Being then the offspring of God." That is the fundamental truth here. We never understand the full and final significance of this great parable until we start there. The man presented to us here is the son of his father. Man is the offspring of God.

Yet perhaps the most flaming revelation of the truth is found in the letter to the Hebrews, almost accidentally and incidentally, so that we hurry over it and miss its profound significance. The writer of the letter says, "We had the fathers of our flesh to chasten us, and we gave them reverence; shall we not much rather be in subjection to the Father of spirits and live?" This is the Christian philosophy revealed. "The fathers of our flesh...the Father of spirits." No man is the father of the spirit of his child. He is only the father of the flesh. That is what Wordsworth meant, in spite of all criticism of him, when he said, "Trailing clouds of glory do we come From God Who is our home."

It is when we see that truth about ourselves and humanity generally that we begin to understand what sin is. That is clearly revealed as we look at this picture which Jesus drew. The facts then revealed are these. Man is offspring of God. His being is due to the Divine action. Our being is His. Our likeness is His. Our possibilities are His. We have no power which He has not created. The only thing in us which He did not create is the paralysis which prevents the use of power. The only thing in us which He did not create is the poison which makes it impossible to come to realization of all the meaning of our lives. When the writing appeared upon the wall of the banqueting hall of the ancient king, and the prophet interpreted it, the supreme charge made against the voluptuous drunken Belshazzar was, "The God in Whose hand thy breath is, and Whose are all thy ways, hast thou not glorified." Man's likeness in the deepest fact of his personality is a likeness to God, though the image be marred beyond recognition by any except God Himself. He sees the likeness, and all the possibilities are God-created, whether material, mental, moral, or spiritual. Whatever use men may be making of them, they are part of the Divine origin and creation. Let it be said bluntly, the devil never made a blade of grass. He has destroyed much. He never created a capacity. He is always aiming at the destruction of the material, mental, or spiritual. Every power has come from God; the physical which enables us to see, to hear, to touch; the mental, enabling us to think, calculate, and arrange; the spiritual, that haunting inner sense that awakes in every man ever and anon, surprisingly, telling him he is more than flesh, but fire.

With that fundamental fact of relationship in mind, we find next the story of separation. What a story it is! The son came to his father and said to him, "Give me the portion of thy substance that falleth to me." The word there means *being*, all the things that make for being. What made him say that to his father? The request was a revelation of the fact that he had lost confidence in his father. There was in his mind an idea that his father stood between him and something that he supremely desired, which he considered would be better for him than the things it was possible for him to have in the father's house, and under the father's restraint.

That is the old story according to this Book. That is how sin entered human life in the Garden. The enemy suggested that God was holding something back. "Yea, hath God said?" Well, it is not so. Take that, and you shall be as gods. God is keeping back from you something, a god-like quality which you ought to have. That was the devil's voice, and that is what this young fellow felt. That is the whole tragedy of sin. That is what is the mater with humanity. "Give me the portion of thy substance that falleth to me"; and his father gave him what he asked.

Then came the voluntary act. He decided to act alone. He decided to leave for the far country, and the farther the better. He would break away from restraint, the law of the father's house, these requirements of his father's house. He went far from home, far from love, far from restraint, and he went away from what he did not recognize at the moment, the guidance that would help him in any crisis.

That is the story of sin. While not denying the fact of our relationship to the race and the fact of racial sin; I would insist that we may so place the emphasis upon that fact of racial sin a to miss the fact of personal wrong-doing and sin. What is the matter with men today? They are away, and have gone as far away from God as they can, even though there may be some who recognize Him with certain gestures, when in all the actualities of their lives they are managing for themselves. So far is that true I may quote a common saying, which is banal in its commonplaceness and tragic in its revelation. Some man is pointed out to me, apparently a great success in the world, and I am told he is a self-made man. What a stupid lie it is. No man is self-made originally, and no man is self-made, whatever the position he may have made for himself. Many years ago a man came to see me after a service, and said to me, "I am interested in all you have said, but I do not believe a word of it." When a man talks like that, it is better than anyone who says he believes, when he does not believe at all. This man said, "You tell me I ought to worship God." Then he said this amazing thing: "I have nothing to thank God for." In a moment like that, when we are startled out of our own common sense, one is given something to say. I looked at him, and I said, "Is that so? Are you a strong man?" "Oh yes," he replied, "I am." I said to him, "Ho much have you spent on doctor's bills lately?" "Not a penny." "And yet you have nothing to thank God for?" He might have said as many others might say, "My health is due to my own care." Oh, fools and blind. Every breath we draw, we draw in God's air and exhale. If man poisons it, and we get poisoned because man has poisoned it, that's another matter. We cannot live without the ability to breathe. We cannot live without God's water. I can live very well without water man has poisoned, but I cannot live without water. It is God's world, and God's gifts are bestowed upon us. The trouble is we have taken them, and have said we can manage them for ourselves, and we do not want God.

That is all very well at first. I can almost believe that the journey into the far country was rather a pleasant one. He felt it rather good to be free. A damnably luring and deceptive word oftentimes, but that is what he felt. In going, he had put himself outside home and love, restriction and guidance. That is the story of human sin, of yours and mine. He was a son, but a son who had formed a wrong opinion about his father, and had a false conceit of himself. This is not a lonely story. It is the story of all sin.

Here we leave our first study. Oh that I had the voice to say to all the little children what was expressed in the words of Longfellow to them.

Stay, stay at home, my heart, and rest;
Home-keeping hearts are happiest,
For those who wander they know not where,
Are full of trouble and full of care;
To stay at home is best.

Weary and homesick, and distressed;
They wander east, they wander west,
And are baffled, and beaten, and blown about
By the winds of the wilderness of doubt;
To stay at home is best.
Then stay at home, my heart, and rest;

The bird is safest in its nest;
O'er all that flutter their wings and fly
A hawk is hovering in the sky;
To stay at home is best.

Or if I speak to the youth and the maiden who have gone beyond childhood: Are you in the far country, dear lad, dear maiden? Are you there? How did you come there? Have you prayed recently? Have you worshipped? Are you acknowledging God, and yielding to His holy and beneficent requirements? How did you get into the far country? Somewhere you doubted God, and made a bid for freedom, believing, though perhaps you never formulated a belief in God, that you could manage it. Or are you in the far country because father and mother never told you these things? That is the tragedy of all tragedies. There are fathers who feed their children and educated them, and amuse them, and do nothing else; and they are surprised when the child breaks away not only from their restraint, but so as to bring tragedy, disaster, and ruin upon himself or herself. Did your parents never tell you?

Well, if you are in the far country, go back home before the depths are reached. There is no necessity to go as far as this young man did, that you should reach the uttermost depravity before turning back home.

Somewhere there is a man or woman who has spent all, someone who is in want in the land of plenty, someone who has known famine, who has been hungry, and no man has given to you. You are in the far country, destitute. What shall I say to you? Go on and finish the story. See what this man did, and do the same. See how the father received the returning son. Though the road be long, the Father is hastening on the way to meet you, and ere you have had time to make yourself presentable, the Father's kiss is on your cheek, and His arms are about you. Robe, ring, and sandals await the lost one.

CHAPTER 2

FEEDING SWINE

There he wasted his substance with riotous living. And when he had spent all, there arose a mighty famine in that country; and he began to be in want. And he went and joined himself to one of the citizens of that country; and he sent him into the fields to feed swine. And he would fain have been filled with the husks that the swine did eat; and no man gave unto him (Luke 15:13-16).

THAT is the story of descent to the depths. Happy is the man who discovers his folly soon, and goes back home. For such there need be no fathoming of the depths. I have sometimes thought we preachers have been in danger of preaching as though the Gospel was only for the utterly degraded and depraved. Thank God it is for that man; but there is no need that any one should reach those uttermost depths of degradation. There is no premium to be placed upon vulgar sin. Happy is the man who early discovers the folly of attempting to govern his own life by taking his substance from God, and wasting it in the far country; and discovering his folly, turns his face homeward and receives the welcome of his father.

In these brief and pregnant sentences, our Lord has shown what the ultimate result is of leaving home, of turning one's back upon the

Father, upon God; and going away from His restriction to the far country. It is one of the most marvellous pictures in literature.

Some people are old enough to remember some pictures drawn by William Hogarth, called "The Rake's Progress." In them, in a striking way, Hogarth portrayed a man in surroundings of culture, elegance, and wealth breaking away, and in the series of pictures, he showed him descending until he is at last seen in the gutter. They were very striking pictures; but for a presentation of the truth, while Hogarth's inspiration was in this story, the pictures fell far short of the amazing revelation of what that degradation means, which is to be found in these sentences of Jesus. There are multitudes of people in the world today who are not down in the gutter. They have never passed through the material experiences that rob them of everything, and they are not down in that sense. Hogarth's picture would not portray them at all. But they are in the gutter. They are away from God. They are as desolate as that man whom Hogarth pictured; and our Lord with that finality of teaching which was always His—for never man spake as He spoke—has given us simple sentences, one succeeding the other, sketching briefly, graphically, forcefully, the downward course, until the ultimate depths are reached.

Leaving out much of the verbiage, read again the seven-fold description in short phrases. "He wasted his substance." "He spent all." "There arose a mighty famine." "He began to be in want." "He was sent to feed swine." "He would fain have been filled with the husks." "No man gave unto him." That is the whole story, and it applies not only to such a one as Hogarth pictured in his remarkable sketches; but to humanity anywhere, where humanity has turned its back upon God, and sought for enfranchisement within its own will and government. We will glance at those sentences. It is the story of declivity, and yet every stage is an experience, and the whole is full of force and suggestiveness.

First, when he reached the far country, what did he do? "He wasted his substance with riotous living." That is so simple. If we are not careful, we do not grasp the significance of it. What is waste? I think it may be defined simply and sufficiently as disbursement of possessions without adequate return; to take the substance of life, and expend it in such a way as to squander it without any abiding satisfaction or proper return. "He wasted his substance with riotous living." There is really a repetition here, for the word riotous means without saving. He took the gifts the father bestowed upon him, and in the far county he spent them, and by their spending made no provision for the leaner days, and the ultimate needs of life. Paul uses the same word, in effect, when he said, "Be not drunken with wine wherein is riot, but be filled with the Spirit." Riotous living is wasteful living, the scattering of forces that bring back no return. That is the first thing we read about this man.

What did he waste? "His substance." He had been to his father and had said, "Give me the portion of thy substance that falleth to me"; and his father had given him what he asked. He had come into possession of gifts from his father. So man is seen here going out from God to waste his substance, *His* substance. The root idea of the word *substance* is that of being; all the forces from God that make life. All the forces that are being expended today in iniquity and wickedness are Divine forces prostituted, squandered. Man has nothing in that sense that he has not received form God. At the back of the loaf the snowy flour, the mill, and the miller, and the farmer; and at the back of him, God. "Give us this day our daily bread," and we cannot get it save from God. All man's resources are Divine gifts, all his material resources. I have been in this world over the threescore years. For those years, I have been breathing its air, eating its food provided for me. All my material life, all the powers with which God has so wondrously blessed me through the years, they are His. What have I done with them? They are gone beyond recall. I cannot call back a single ounce of energy I have expended. What have I done with them? I am only asking the question.

Or pass from the physical to the mental, the posers of thought, observation, comparison, deduction; all the wonderful mental activities of a human life. These have been spent for what, and with what result?

Or rise to a higher level, and think of moral considerations, that admiration of goodness and hatred of evil which is common to all humanity, however depraved. There is no roué in our great city who does not know in his deepest heart the beauty of goodness. What has been done with these moral conceptions?

Or finally, those spiritual forces that ever and anon bring us vision, and a sense of the larger, the vaster, the eternal. What have we done with them? What are the returns from this expenditure of substance?

That is the test for every life. Have we anything resulting from our expenditure of these forces, of which we can say, "This is the result, and this will abide, whatever else may perish"? There was satire in the word of the old Hebrew prophet, addressed to the people of God, "Ye have sold yourselves for naught." A man may say, I have done very well, I have made my fortune. What is your fortune? What has it gotten for you? What do you possess? Do you possess it? Oh no, you do not possess it. A few short years at the very most and your hand will not sign cheques [checks], you will be a dead hand upon future generations, and men will fling it off sooner or later. We go on living, spending our powers, material, mental, moral, and spiritual; and when we take stock, there is no balance, there is nothing left, nothing we can hold, nothing of which we can say, "It is ours." Remember what Jesus said to His own disciples, "Lay not up for yourselves treasures upon the earth, where moth and rust doth consume, and where thieves break through and steal, but lay up for yourselves treasures in heaven." Have we any treasures laid up there? A man who has turned his back upon God has none. He is bounded by the present. His gold has brought him no return so far as his output of energy is concerned. He has wasted his substance.

Mark how it is immediately followed by the second phrase. "When he had spent all." That is the inevitable issue of waste. The hour of utter extremity arrives when the capital is all gone, and when a man has no argosies on the seas which presently will be returning, bringing him the returns for his expenditure. "When he had spent all." Waste will bring every man there sooner or later in some form. I need not stress the physical. No one can take the physical forces and abuse them and waste them and scatter them without weakening them. Our hospitals are full of such cases. No one can take mental powers and misuse them without ruining them until they cease to act. Our mental asylums are full proof of that. Moral powers cannot be denied. The moral consciousness which forgets the perpetual necessity for reconstruction and renewal of fellowship with God presently becomes dead. There are some terrible expressions in the New Testament, "A dead conscience," "A conscience seared as with a hot iron," that is a conscience that has lost its sensitiveness. When this man began his life by voluntary separation from God, and went to the far country, there went with him a moral consciousness that made him blush when he told a lie, that made him feel awkward when he heard or told a story that brushed the bloom of modesty fro the cheek of youth; but he has lost the power to blush, and is impure without sense of awkwardness today. He is a wreck. He has spent all.

Immediately we pass to the next phrase. "There arose a mighty famine in that land." I do not believe that Jesus meant that when he had spent all there came a famine that had not existed before, but that to the man who had spent all there arose a mighty famine. There is famine everywhere when men have spent all, physically and materially. London, or any city, is the home of famine to the man who has nothing. If a man has spent all physically, the city of plenty is the city of famine and destitution. There is nothing in the far country when a man has run through Divinely bestowed gifts. The far country has no currency of its own. A man can only get out of it as he puts into it. A man may say, "I am getting a great deal out of the far country, laughter and merriment. I am having what the world calls a good time. I am seeing life." All the things you are getting out you are putting in, the things with which God has endowed you. Spend them apart from His control and presently, in the midst of laughter, you will be in agony; in the midst of plenty, you will be dying of hunger. There was a mighty famine when he had spent all. As long as he had anything to spend there was no famine; but Oh, my masters, when material strength has gone, mental forces are wasted, the moral sense is dead, and the spirit vision ended; then famine follows. "There arose a mighty famine in that country."

"And he began to be in want." Although we are tracing the story of this man's descent to the depths, I see here the first gleam of hope, but this man is by no means at the end of the darkness. "He began to be in want." The first sense of the distance of the far country broke upon him. When a man begins to be in want, he will try, for all he is worth, to deny his want. Sometimes he will try to cover it with flippancy, sometimes with cynicism, sometimes with professed agnosticism. Behind much of the flippancy of some people, and the cynicism of others, and the agnosticism with all its flaunting imperiousness, there lies the hunger of the soul which the man is trying to cover up, and refuses to acknowledge.

That sense often makes a man take refuge in prolonged rebellion. That is seen here in this story. When this man began to be in want, he went and joined himself to a citizen of the far country. Why did he not go home? Men do not do that. They prolong their return. They will not go back at once. This man had hardly begun to think seriously about the things he had left at home, so he joined himself to a citizen of the far country into which he had gone.

The next word is that the citizen "sent him into his fields to feed swine." We can only get the full impact of this statement in the light of the outlook of the country in which the words were spoken, and in the light of the fact that Jesus was addressing Himself to Hebrews, to the rulers, the Pharisees and scribes. He used an expression that to them meant the uttermost degradation. This man was not going home. He joined himself to a citizen, and what will the citizen do? Send him into his fields to feed swine. He prolonged his degradation; indeed, he deepened his degradation. That was the estimate of the citizen of the far country of this man's worth. Go and feed my swine. The whole picture becomes powerfully graphic.

We can translate it into the language of today, and into some experiences we have seen and watched. There is a public-house loafer yonder! He is an Oxford graduate, but there is nothing he does but hang round for a pint of beer and a chuck out! One of the most appalling and tragic experiences of my life was the memory of a preacher of marvellous power, under whose spell men sat with wonder and amazement; and the last thing I knew of that man was that in a public-house he was preaching an old sermon for the amusement of the crowd, and the payment of half a pint of beer. You say, my friend, young man, I am never coming to that. How do you know? Do you suppose he ever meant to come to that? In an evil hour, he took his substance, and began to forget the government of God, and wandered until he had spent all, and then the citizen of the far country sent him to feed swine. That is the abiding application of the story.

Then what? "He began to be in want." Not only did he begin to be in want, but "he would fain have been filled with the husks that the swine did eat." Here we are face to face with the tragedy of the spiritual, the hunger of soul. Let us quickly add the last sentence of all, "No man gave unto him." That is the story. Their only interest in him was that as a machine for feeding their pigs. Each for himself! If he fails, let him die. That is all the far country has for any man. He has spent his substance, and is in want. The deepest hunger of his life is asserting itself. The far county has nothing to give. "No man gave unto him." Why not? Because in this realm of the material, the law of the survival of the fittest is the only law. Spend the forces of life without reference to God in the midst of riotous companionships, in ways of wickedness, gaining o return, having no reserve, and presently when all is gone, famine will come, and hunger is there. The far country will give nothing, will have no pity, no sympathy, no help. Shall I surprise you when I say that the law of the survival of the fittest is an excellent one? It is one that obtains through all life. Why should failure be perpetuated? Is it not wholly beneficent that the world will have no wastrels?

But that is not the story in its finality. There is Someone Who will give, if no man gave unto Him. The only basis upon which God saves a man is that he shall be remade. While the world's method of flinging out the man who has wasted his substance is wholly beneficent, we thank God for the evangel. Take the Gospel away, and there is no hope for such a man, because the world cannot feed him, or reconstruct him, or remake him. It has no philosophy that is equal to it, no force that can accomplish it; and therefore the best thing it can do is to let him die, lest he spoil other lives.

Thank God there is One Who came to seek and save the lost. Over against this wholly beneficent and Divine principle of the survival of the fittest, we have the great message of salvation, the remaking of the individual. Let the law of the survival of the fittest work itself out in heartlessness and brutality as it seems, until the man be flung on to the world's scrap-heap; then, thank God, there is One Who comes and puts His hand upon that scrap-heap, takes hold of the rubbish, and makes it again. That is the Gospel. He can make the desert blossom as the rose. He can take the wrecked, ruined, burnt-out, and spoiled life and remake it, and ere His work is done, He will present it faultless before the throne of God. He is watching over the sinner, waiting for his home-coming, running already upon the rough road to meet him, to place upon his cheek the kiss of eternal pardon.

CHAPTER 3

RETURNING HOME

But when he came to himself he said, How many hired servants of my father's have bread enough and to spare, and I perish here with hunger! I will arise and go to my father, and will say unto him, Father, I have sinned against heaven, and in thy sight: I am no more worthy to be called thy son: Make me as one of thy hired servants (Luke 15:17-19).

W E have followed this man to the far county, and have seen him pass to the depths. We have seen in him a revelation of humanity in its definite break with God. He left his father. He attempted to escape from the restrictions of his father's house. He went out feeling that he could manage his own affairs better that his father could; and he travelled away—significant phrase—to the "far country"; a long way off, for his purpose, the further the better.

We have seen him descending to the depths through those processes which, in simple and yet sublime and searching sentences, our Lord employed. We saw him wasting his substance with riotous living. We saw him conscious of famine that arose in the land. We saw him brought to the place of absolute penury. Then we saw him still persisting in an independent attitude, joining himself to a citizen of the far country. We have seen the estimate that citizen had of him. He sent him into his fields to feed swine. So we have followed him from home to the far country, and have seen him going to the depths.

This study opens with a very significant word; "When he came to himself." Standing at the centre of the story, these words reveal the true meaning of this man's former action, and indicate the way by which he returned. To use the figure, it is a light in the midst of the passage, flashing both ways, illuminating all that we have seen, and revealing so far as this man was concerned, the meaning of all now to be considered.

"When he came to himself." That opens the way to home and restoration. "He came to himself." What does that mean? We can state the whole fact at the beginning in a few sentences. In all the processes in which we saw him going to the far country, and descending to the depths, he was mad, he was beside himself; his actions were characterized by insanity. "But when he came to himself," the contrast is seen immediately. What a change is here, a change in outlook, a change in purpose. All the things that followed that dawn of reason proved that his action from that moment was the action of sanity.

Here then we have a revelation of the insanity of godlessness, and the sanity of godliness. The outsider, the man of the world, often looks upon those living a godly life as being a little short in some ways. When Festus said to Paul, "Paul, thou art mad; thy much learning doth turn thee to madness," he heard him speak of his life and faith and Gospel. The cynical man of the world said he was mad; and that idea still obtains. Perhaps in these days it does not express itself in that way, but there are many people, our friends in the social set, who really think there is something queer about us, that religion is characterized by a certain form of insanity. But the true rationalist—to redeem this word from possible abuse—is the believer, the Christian man, who is living his life in right relationship with God, willingly, submissively. That is the life of reason as well as the life of faith. This man here went down, until he was in the depths; and suddenly reason dawned, and then "he came to himself."

In the simplest way, take that conception and watch this man in the light of it; and in the light of the man's story, look at human life when lived apart from the Father's home and government; in other words, apart from God. All the signs which we associate with insanity on the ordinary plane of life are to be found in the action of this man.

One of the first evidences of insanity is loss of memory. One sign of insanity is that things are forgotten. I need not stay to argue that. In the early days of his sojourn in the far country, this man lived his life thoughtless of his father and his home, and of his relationship to both. That may be a piece of mere speculative interpretation. Then treat the story on its simplest human level, not as a story of nineteen centuries ago, but that of a young man in similar conditions today; one who gathers from his father his share of property, takes his way to another land and spends it. The most surprising thing is that man's forgetfulness of his relationship to his father, and his responsibility to him. It was Carlyle who once declared that the being the devil dreaded the most is the man who dares to think. It is a perfectly true statement. Yet this loss of memory, this life lived in forgetfulness of essential relationships and abiding truths, is the first evidence of insanity.

When they charged Hamlet with being mad, he said:

...Bring me to the test,
And I the matter will reword, which madness
Would gambol from.

In other words, he said, I have not lost my memory; bring me to the test. Here is a Biblical description of the godless life: "All his thoughts are, There is no God." There is a fine, subtle irony in that word. The thoughts of the godless man are characterized by forgetfulness of God; through all his life, in his thinking, planning, arranging. Jesus drew another picture of this life in another parable, that of the rich fool; the man who lived in the midst of fertile fields, and in prosperity, and said, "My fruits, my barns my corn, my goods"; until like a crack of thunder comes the arresting word, "But God said unto him, Thou foolish one, this night is thy soul required of thee." Are we living there? The recitation of the creed on Sunday is no proof that God is remembered; or joining in the worship of the sanctuary, if God is referred to in a restless hour of irksome worship on the Sabbath. If He be forgotten on six days, it is the first alarming evidence of spiritual insanity, and the wearisome and empty performance on the seventh is of no value.

But another evidence of madness is that of having distorted views, so that certain persons are mistaken for others. In that masterly delineation of madness in Shakespeare's *King Lear*, the king could not tell the difference between Edgar and the fool, and attributed to the fool all wisdom, and to Edgar all folly. Nothing is more sad than to go through the mournful wards or corridors of an insane asylum and see those who have lost their reason, imagining that they are someone else, not understanding things, and having a false view altogether. There was a man who upon one occasion said he was Julius Caesar, and at another time he changed his mind, and declared he was Napoleon Bonaparte! Distorted views. This man taking his journey to the far country, the thought of his heart was expressed in the action of his life. In his heart he thought of his father as being hard and unkind; and of those men he will meet in the far country as being generous and kind. These were distorted views indeed. He was ignorant of himself and of his father. He was mad.

Take another note of madness here: his inability to appreciate relative values. I look at the things he gives, and examine what he gets, and I see at once this man had lost his sense of relative values. Everything must be tested by that standard in the matter of bartering. If I see children playing by the roadside, exchanging in their play beads for beads, beads of glass, crystal green, red, blue, that is fine. But if I saw them bartering beads for jewels, diamonds, sapphires, emeralds, and rubies, I should say there was something wrong here; it is a sign of insanity, though the children might not have known what they were doing. One sign of insanity is that we do not know relative values. Here this man is seen turning his back upon home and love and compassion for the companions of the far country, choosing "the pleasures of sin for a season" rather than the pleasures which are at the right hand of God. To do this is to put out of the life all wealth and richness of God's purpose, and to take instead all the beggarly emptiness and poverty of the world.

Again I find in this man's action loss of business acumen. That, every business man will admit, is a sure evidence of insanity. The man who takes his capital and lives on it without investing it, how does it end? There is one short and brutal answer, which tells all the truth—bankruptcy! That is the story here. He received substance from his father. He spent it. He did not invest it. That is the ultimate proof of insanity.

Yet look once again. We have seen his loss of memory, and forgetfulness of his father. What did this really mean? The death of love. If he had not lost the power of love, he never would have wounded the heart of his father as he did. Love was stifled, killed, trampled upon until it was non-existent.

And yet once more, pride, self-satisfaction; the ignorance of madness. This man did not know how mad he was. Is there any madness worse than the madness of such pride, and the unconsciousness of it all? That magnificent independence in which he made his boast is unutterable madness. He was masquerading in the robes of royalty, but was unable to administer the affairs of the kingdom. Can there be anything more mad than that?

So finally, self-destruction, not necessarily immediate. At the back of all his action was lack of recognition of the first law of human life, the law of self-preservation. The surest suicide is the persistent sinner who goes on in his godlessness. Many men commit suicide over whom no coroner pronounces such a verdict. Life is wasted, flung way, expended, issuing in self-destruction.

"But when he came to himself." Everything is at once changed, and as we watch the result, all that follows stands in striking contrast to those notes of madness which we have seen.

"He came to himself," and at once memory reasserted itself. He thought of the old days and the old conditions that he felt were still obtaining there. He thought of that which he had endeavoured to forget. He began to think. My father's house, my father's hired servants, they are not hungry. They are not destitute. There is bread there to spare. These things are becoming real to him again.

His madness had been characterized by distorted views. With the return of the true balance of reason, he comes to right views. Notice how he said again and again, "my father." There is always a threnody in it. There he was in his loneliness and desolation, but he had come to himself, and naming his father as he ought to be named. That is another sign of returning reason when the soul begins to recognize its relation to God, and that "God is love."

In his madness we say that he had no appreciation of relative values. Listen to him as he balanced accounts. It is better to serve at home than to reign here. Freedom here has become slavery. Service there was freedom. I pause here, because it is something many do not believe even today. One of the profoundest words revealing the essence of sin is found in Milton's *Paradise Lost,* words put into the lips of Lucifer, son of the morning, whom he describes as falling from his high estate. They reveal the inwardness of Satan's fall:

> To reign is worth ambition, though in hell;
> Better to reign in hell, than to serve in heaven.

It was a daring thing for Milton to put such a sentiment into Lucifer's lips; and yet how accurate and true it is. Yet that is the supreme evidence that the devil is the ultimate lunatic of the universe, because he does not reign in hell. God reigns in hell. The devil cannot touch a single hair on the back of a single camel that belongs to Job until he has Divine permission; nor can he sift the disciples as wheat. He may think he reigns, but God reigns.

If we take that from the immediate application of the fall of Lucifer, and apply it to a man, it becomes true. No man reigns. He thinks he does. That is his madness, and the return of reason is seen when he comes to the decision that he was wrong, that it would be better to go home and become a hired servant that to live in the far country as he has come to live, and suffer as he has suffered.

Mark also the return of mental acumen. He had taken his capital and spent it, without investing it. He will now go back, not to invest any capital, for he has none to invest; but to invest his own strength, whatever may be left of it, in the service of his father. "Make me as one of thy hired servants." Take my life, and let me serve. It is the return of reason.

Love was coming back. Memory of his father was coming, and humility had come. He was going back to say to his father, "I have sinned." That is one of the most difficult sentences human lips can ever utter. It is quite easy to say we are all sinners. It is a very different thing to say, "I have sinned." It is so in human relationships. There is many a home that never would have been broken up if a man or a woman had dared to say, "I have sinned." That is the language of humility. It is the language of shame. It is the courage of penitence. "I have sinned," I am not worthy. Make me a servant. When reason takes possession of the soul again, a man says immediately, "I have sinned." Humility is the evidence of the dawn of reason.

Finally, in going away to the far country, there was forgetfulness of the first law of life, that of self-preservation. Listen to him. "I perish with hunger! I will arise, and go to my father." In that decision, there is evidence of the return of reason, for he denies himself in order to find himself.

The godless life is the life of madness, insanity. The fashion of the godless world is to think and speak of godly men as those who are lacking in reason. It is the godly life that is rational, the life of sanity. All this is dependent upon the foundation[al] fact of man's peculiar relation to God by first creation. This man was a son. He had relationship with God. To deny that, and have some other view of man, and there is no meaning in all this. If man is only an animal, and has sprung from animal beginning, and has moved up, then I think he has done remarkably well. Only, my masters, there are signs of the reversion to type! The world is full of evidences that man is going back to the slime, to the jungle, to beastliness. This is only an aside, so banish it. We do not believe that of man. We believe in his fall from his high estate; but that he was made in the image and likeness of God; and it is that conception that lies at the back of the this parable.

Have you come to yourself? We have all been taking our substance, and spending it. I do not say we are wasting it. It is gone. What have we to show? Are you conscious of bankruptcy in the spiritual realm, bankruptcy of the fine dignity of personality according to the Divine ideal? Have you come to yourself? Are you beginning to understand that? Stripped of all accidentals, where are you? Are you awaking? Then I tell you, what you need is home, and to get home.

What is the cry of a child
Lost in endless streets, or in stubbled fields forgotten,
Even 'mid forest joys or by ocean's changing wonders?

Surely he cries, his piteous infant accents broken,

"I want to go home!"

What is the cry of a man
Spent with painful toil or with pleasure's vain endeavour,
Maimed with rude buffets dealt by Time's encroaching fingers?

Surely he cries, his quivering tones age-worn and weary,
"I want to go home!"

What is the cry of a soul
Wandering forlorn through straining hosts, unhailed, unheeded,
Lost in a mist of anguish, seeing afar the glory?

Surely it cries, whether young or old, with a bitter wailing
"I want to go home!"

Is anyone saying that? Then there is the remainder of the parable. Start the journey home. Tramp, however hard the way; and ere long you will find the open door, and the Father greeting you. God home!

CHAPTER 4

THE WELCOME HOME

And he arose, and come to his father. But while he was yet afar off, his father saw him, and was moved with compassion, and ran, and fell on his neck, and kissed him. And the son said: Father, I have sinned against heaven, and in thy sight: I am no more worthy to be called thy son. But the father said to his servants, Bring forth quickly the best robe, and put it on him; and put a ring on his hand, and shoes on his feet: and bring forth the fatted calf, and kill it, and let us eat, and make merry: for this my son was dead, and is alive again; he was lost, and is found. And they began to be merry (Luke 15:20-24).

WE now reach the true value of this familiar story. The events we have previously considered have been of value, but after all they have been incidental and preparatory. This has been an unveiling of the departure of humanity from God, and God's attitude toward humanity, as pictured in the rebellious and returning son.

As a story it is natural, simple, human. It is not at all difficult to believe that when Jesus uttered these words, He had some actual father in His mind, some actual son in His thought. We have seen the whole procedure repeated constantly in our own observation. The essential humanity of it appeals to the heart. The finest instincts of men recognize the beauty of the story. That has made it so popular. Everyone knows the story, and no one quarrels with any part of it, until we come to the elder son. Thus the story is in keeping with the whole process of Incarnation wherein Christ came to reveal God to man through Man. Jesus takes a human picture to show us God. He is able to do this because man is the offspring of God.

In glancing over these verses, there are four things to notice. First, the welcome which the returning son received. Secondly, the interrupted prayer which the son offered. Thirdly, the reinstatement which the father made. Finally, we shall take one brief glance at the picture of the home life with which the story ends.

Look first at his welcome. We can add nothing to the actual words, but consider these marvellous sentences. "While he was yet afar off his father saw him." He had gone to the far country. He was coming back from that far country; but while he was still afar off his father saw him. Take the human story. May we not be sure that his father had been watching for him, and never forgotten him, had never given him up. How often the eyes of the old man had rested upon that highway, or had looked toward the distant hills; and at last he saw his son coming, saw him afar off, and knew him. He was changed, probably he was literally in rags, possibly unkempt, haggard. I wonder if anyone else would have recognized him so far off, except his father.

That is the first thing to be noticed. The lesson is that God is ever watching and waiting for the home-coming of those who in rebellion against Him have taken their substance and wandered away, and wasted it in riotous living. God is always watching, waiting for their home-coming, and no scars of sin can efface the image of God from the eyes of God. Oh yes, the scars of sin can efface the image of God from the eyes of men. We have seen human faces in which it would be very difficult to trace any likeness to the Divine image. We could not see it, but God could see it. He sees beneath all the disfigurement, all the bruising, the marring, the battering, the Divine likeness. When the boy was far off, when the father first saw him, almost unrecognizable, the father knew him.

There comes back to me an illustration, the story of a Scotch lassie, who broke away from home and restraint. She went to the far country, and fell into sin, terrible sin, and went down to the depths until she was derelict; and like this boy, she had nothing left. Ruined in every way, she traced her way back home, and arrived at her mother's cottage in the night. When she came up the winding lane that led to the cottage, she was amazed to see a light shining in the window in the middle of the night. She trembled, and feared that her mother was ill. She quickened her footsteps, noticed that the door of the cottage was open, and then paused. Her mother heard her footsteps, and knew them, and swiftly she ran down the stairs to her lassie. "Mother, what is the matter? Why is the door open? What is the light burning for?" "Janie, that light has never been out of a night nor the door shut since you went away!" Motherhood, Fatherhood, God. "His father saw him," he knew him.

Go on to the next sentence. I cannot add anything to this. He "was moved with compassion." At this point in the story I am always inclined to be critical, looking at it as a human story merely. When this old man saw his son, he started running to meet him. Such action seems at first to be characterized by an utter absence of dignity. "He ran." Yet look again! Absence of dignity? I tell you it was the demonstration of complete dignity because it was inspired by compassion. He was moved with pity, and he ran. As the prophet said, "A God ready to pardon." All the superficialities of false dignity are submerged and swept aside, and in the dignity of a great love he ran to meet his boy.

Let us reverently climb from the illustration as Christ intended that we should. This is Christ's picture of God. I dare not have drawn such a picture, or made such a suggestion. I believe in a God holy, high, eternal, Who occupies the throne from everlasting to everlasting. These human eyes have been so accustomed to associate with that throne an authority and a dignity which bends with difficulty. But He Who shares that throne has drawn it and says, "If you would know, son of God wandering in the far country, wasting your substance, remembering God with breaking heart, how you will be received if you return to Him, then this is the picture. God runs to meet you with an eagerness born of His compassion."

What next? He "fell on his neck, and he smothered him with kisses." That is it. He kissed him very much. Hold on! I am inclined to stand back, and to be critical. I look at the picture and say, "Is not that a sign of weakness?" Dismiss the thought. It was a sign of strength. Would it not have been better to wait until the boy had made acknowledgment of his wrong-doing? No, he knew his boy. He knew that the boy would make his confession best when his head was pillowed upon his father's breast. He did not wait for him to be cleansed. He put his arms round the boy's neck, smothered him with kisses that marked reconciliation and pardon, tokens that in the father's heart he was reinstated immediately, seeing he had set his face towards home, and had tramped the long distance, and had arrived there.

That is a wonderful picture of the sure impression of the love of God made upon the spirit of man when he comes back to God. Perhaps those who have been furthest away understand it best. They come back to find a forgiveness that also forgets. Do not miss that. We may say,

"Can God forget anything?" Yes, in this sense, "Thy sins and thine iniquities will I remember against thee no more for ever." Yes, a forgiveness in that sense forgets. That is so different to us. Somebody says, I have forgiven that man, but I shall never forget his wrong-doing. That is why we are so unlike God. Such a man who says that must be related to the elder son! God forgives, and God forgets.

Now listen to the interrupted prayer. To understand it we must go back to read again the previous verses. He had said to himself in the far country, "I will arise and go to my father, and will say unto him, Father I have sinned against heaven, and in thy sight; I am no more worthy to be called thy son; make me as one of thy hired servants." That is the prayer. But notice he never got through it. Listen to him, "I have sinned against heaven and in thy sight; I am no more worthy to be called thy son"; and at that point the father broke in upon the prayer, interrupted it, ended it. He intended to say, "I have sinned, I have forfeited my rights; let my degradation continue. I do not ask to be reinstated as a son. Let me atone for what I have done by what I will do. Let me serve. Let me wipe out the sin and shame of the years in which I have wasted substance, wounded thy heart, by going without sandals, by being a slave in thy household. I have learned that it is better to serve at home than to reign in the far country." But he had no time to finish. He never got the chance to say, "Make me as one of thy hired servants." He had said enough. He had said the thing necessary to say—"I have sinned." To take the Greek word and put it into common language, I have missed the mark. What I thought was right was wrong. What I thought was liberty was slavery. It was necessary that he should say, "I have sinned, I am no more worthy to be called thy son." Past sin leaves its effect. I have forfeited all my rights. Pride was humbled, shame was experienced, and confession was made. But he never got any further.

This was not impertinent repentance, saying, I have made my acknowledgment, and now it is your business to reinstate me. He was permitted to say another thing, "I am no longer worthy to be called thy son." This man took his position on his father's breast, not because he dared to seek that position, but because grace had placed him there in infinite love. His degradation was not in the will of his father. It was not the father's will that he had gone away, and now he would not perpetuate the boy's wrong-doing. Menial service will not atone. The service of tomorrow will never atone for the sin of yesterday.

This is where so many people make a mistake. At the beginning of the year, we make good resolutions. I am not against such resolutions. Someone has said the way to hell is paved with good intentions. But so is the way to heaven. Resolutions may be quite good. We say we are going to turn over a new leaf. What a curious figure of speech that is. What do we mean? We mean—we have sinned, we have blotted the page, and have smirched the escutcheon. Here is the record up to now, and it is blotted as badly as can be. We turn over a new leaf. What is to be done with those leaves we have turned over? We cannot undo them. We cannot blot them out. Nothing can be done when that new leaf is turned over to put right the wrong done, and right the record of the past pages of the years. It is no use turning over a new leaf in that way. The probability is we shall do as badly on the new one as the old. No, don't turn over a new leaf. Take a new book from the pierced Hand, put your hand in His, and as my mother did when she taught me to write, she held my hand, let Him hold your hand as you write the story. We cannot, by service, undo anything of the past. The Father does not ask it. He will break in upon your prayer.

But there is no need. What will the father say? "Bring forth quickly the best robe, and put it on him, and put a ring on his hand and shoes on his feet." The prayer was interrupted because there was infinite provision made for the reception of the son through the compassion of the father's heart. Not by what he can do can the son atone, but by that which is done for him, apart from him; and by that which is done for him, apart from him; and by that which is made over to him in infinite grace, atonement is made.

Do not forget that this part of the parable is not complete in itself. That we saw in our first study. The three parts of the parable reveal the truth, or rather, three phases of the parable. The first is that of the shepherd, the second that of the woman who seeks. All the method by which grace operates is not revealed in this single aspect of the parable; but the fact is made perfectly clear that provision for the reception of the son is made, not by the son, but by the father, and that it is bestowed upon the son out of the exceeding grace of the father's heart.

Finally, let us take a brief glance at that provision. Here again we get back to the simplicities which are symbols of sublimities. Put the best robe on him, and a ring on his finger and shoes on his feet. Robe, ring, and royal sandals await the lost one. These three things answer exactly the prayer which he meant to have prayed. The robe is the answer to "I have sinned." The ring is the answer to "I am no more worthy to be called thy son." The sandals constitute the answer to "Make me one of thy hired servants." These symbols are Eastern. Put the robe on him, the robe that befits the father's house. Perhaps it is necessary to stay here to notice that the best robe was not put on over the rags, the filthy garments. Some would speak as though the robe of righteousness was put over the sinner's rags to hide them. God is not unclean!

There is no doubt a cleansing preceded the robing in the case of this son.

The ring was the sign of relationship, of sonship. "Put a ring on his finger." He is my son. Give him the sign of sonship. By that token, give him authority to become a son. So there is not only atonement, but regeneration, and reinstatement by that infinite miracle. Put a ring on his finger; bring him back into the relationship that he had forfeited and lost by his sin.

What else? Put shoes on his feet. Still the picture is Eastern. The slave was never permitted to wear shoes. The badge of slavery was the absence of sandals. When Paul was writing of the equipment of the Christian, he said, "Your feet shod with the preparation of the Gospel of peace"; that is, equipment for service, not the service of a slave, but of a son. Robe, ring, and royal sandals await the lost one.

One final glance at the home. While not desiring to be controversial, there are some who tell us if we introduce atonement and sacrifice into this story, it will have to be re-written, for that does not appear here. The first answer to that objection is that if so, the whole of the New Testament will have to be re-written. The second answer is that this story is only one-third of the parable. The parable is a threefold one. It opens with the story of the shepherd, and:

> None of the ransomed ever knew
> How deep were the waters crossed;
> Nor how dark was the night that the Lord passed through
> Ere He found His sheep that was lost.

That is the part of the parable of God, in His Son, ransoming the sinner.

Yet I am not sure that we are correct in saying there is nothing about sacrifice here. The late Professor Samuel Ives Curtiss wrote a valuable book on Semitic religions, the outcome of his personal investigation in the Holy Land of the manners and customs of the people. In the course of it, he described how when a young man had been away from home in a distant land, whether as a prodigal or a traveller, on his return it was the custom to offer on the threshold a sacrifice, which sacrifice became the feast of welcome. That is exactly what you find here. In conversation with Dr. Curtiss, I asked him if he had ever applied that custom to the parable of the prodigal son. He said he had never thought of that relationship, but admitted that it was a most interesting thought. This makes it the more valuable. Before this son could get back into his home, sacrifice was necessary, in case there had been sin. "Bring forth the fatted calf and kill it, and let us eat." This was the very language which would be understood by all Semitic people.

Do not miss that word "merry." There was a meal, and merriment, merriment in the home, not that of the far country. There "the pleasures of sin for a season," but now merriment, gladness, assuredly, and dancing. "Let us be merry." Why? My son, as to himself, was dead; now he is alive. As to my own heart, as though the father had said: he was lost, but now he is found.

Yes, there is that dark background of the elder son. He is never called the elder brother in the parable. Of course he was a brother, but the word is applied to the younger son, and not to the elder. What did he hear? Music and dancing; actual, positive, glorious merriment. We are going to leave him severely alone. It should be remembered that our Lord was talking to a little group of scribes and Pharisees, who had criticized Him as they said, "This Man receiveth sinners, and eateth with them." They knew so much about God, but they did not know God. So we dismiss him, and you also, if you are related to him!

There is only one question for us to ask. Thank God for all who have come home, who have received the robe and ring and sandals. Is there anyone in the far country, or tramping the way home, half-wistfully wondering what is going to happen, and who is prepared to make amends by service. Take this story, and remember He knows; He has seen you; He is running to meet you. May there be a meeting between the returning wanderer and God now.

CHAPTER 5

THE COMPLETION OF THE PARABLE.
A SEQUEL

And He spake unto them this parable, saying, What man of you having a hundred sheep, and having lost one of them, doth not leave the ninety and nine in the wilderness, and go after that which is lost, until he find it? And when he hath found it, he layeth it on his shoulders, rejoicing. And when he cometh home, he calleth together his friends and his neighbours, saying unto them, Rejoice with me, for I have found my sheep which was lost. I say unto you, that even so there shall be joy in heaven over one sinner that repenteth, more than over ninety and nine righteous persons, which need no repentance.

Or what woman having ten pieces of silver, if she lose one piece, doth not light a lamp, and sweep the house, and seek diligently until she find it? And when she hath found it, she calleth together her friends and neighbours, saying, Rejoice with me, for I have found the piece which I had lost. Even so, I say unto you, there is joy in the presence of the angels of God over one sinner that repenteth (Luke 15:3-10).

THIS study is complementary to the four previous ones on the prodigal son. The first ten verses of the chapter contain the first two phases of the one answer of Jesus to the criticism of the scribes and Pharisees.

To understand these two phases, it is necessary to go back into the previous chapter in which Luke has told the story of the presence of our Lord in the house of one of the rulers of the Pharisees. There His words had been characterized by almost severity. Then, turning from the place where He had been a guest, He spoke some of the sternest words that ever passed His lips concerning the terms of discipleship, and explained the reason of the severity of His terms by the figure of the building of a tower, and the conduct of a warfare; ending all by this most searching word, spoken to all men contemplating following Him, and making Him Lord. "Salt, therefore, is good; but even if the salt have lost its savour, where-with shall it be seasoned? It is fit neither for the land nor for the dunghill; men cast it out." Savourless salt, men cast it out!

We notice the close connection between the last words of that severe discourse, in which He demanded new attention to all that He had been saying, with the affirmation of the first verse of the next chapter. "He that hath ears to hear, let him hear. Now all the publicans and sinners were drawing near unto Him for to hear Him." There is striking relationship between these two verses. In spite of the severity of His terms, the publicans and sinners drew near to hear Him. The men most conscious of sin were those most eager to listen to the voice of unqualified holiness. But there were other men standing round, the scribes and Pharisees, who murmured and complained, and they did so in these words; "This Man receiveth sinners, and eateth with them."

Let us at once admit that had He been such as they were, the philosophy underlying their criticism was perfectly correct, and the criticism justified. They meant to say, "If this Man makes Himself the familiar friend of sinning men, He will Himself become a sinner." As they saw Him receiving into familiar friendship men notoriously sinful, they believed what some of us were taught when we were children: You cannot touch pitch without being defiled. Show me your friends, and I will foretell your future.

Our Lord answered their philosophy by giving them a revelation of His personality, and an explanation of His purpose in the one parable in three, the parable of lost things.

To read this parable aright we must bear in mind that it was spoken in answer to criticism, and by it He rebuked these men for a false outlook upon sinning men, and for attempting to compress Him within the narrow compass of their own philosophy. By an unveiling of Himself, and a revelation of the real meaning of His mission in the world, He gave the explanation of why He received sinning men, which caused astonishment and a stumbling block to the scribes and Pharisees. As I watch the process of that unveiling, I see that He rebuked them, not principally for their failure to understand Him, but for their failure to understand the value of sinning men to the heart of God. In this parable we have His reply to that criticism. They said, "This Man receiveth sinners, and eateth with them." He replied, "What man of you, having a hundred sheep, and having lost one of them, doth not leave the ninety and nine in the wilderness, and go after that which is lost until he find it?" His meaning is self-evident. You criticise Me, as though He had said, for sitting and eating with sinners. I do it because they are lost sheep, and I am seeking them.

Then when He came to the second phase of the story, He introduced a new tone, thought, and emphasis, that of the motherly element. He went straight on. There is no break between the two phases, that of the lost sheep, and the woman sweeping and searching and finding, and the father. In the third phase of the parable there does not seem to be the same pertinent application to the criticism of the Pharisees; but we find at the conclusion that the elder son becomes the picture of their attitude. It is important that we should see the sweep of the study before examining some of the details.

There they stood round about Him; the throng of publicans and sinners, smirched men, soiled women. There He stood in the midst of them, talking to them quite familiarly; in all the expressiveness of the Greek word, receiving them unto Himself, into close, familiar comradeship, content to sit down to eat with them, violating all Pharisaic traditions, even without washing His hands. Again, there stand the scribes and Pharisees, the interpreters of the moral law, the teachers of purity, holiness, and righteousness, shocked at His familiarity with sinning men, saying, "This Man receiveth sinners, and eateth with them."

Out of the midst of His comradeship with sinners, He explains and defends His action. He does what He so often did, makes them the judges. Which *of you*, if a sheep was lost, would not find it? Perhaps beyond the circle of inquiring, critical Pharisees were some women listening. Or what woman, had she lost a piece of silver, would not find it by searching? Then He told the story of the younger son, ending with the picture of the elder son, out of sympathy with his father's heart, and unable to welcome the sinning brother home. The criticism of the Pharisees has been transmuted by this parabolic answer of Jesus into the Gospel for the world.

The relation of these three parts of the one parable is evident. Here are the points of unity; the lost things, the sheep, the piece of silver, and the son. The found things, the sheep was found and brought back to the fold. The lost drachma was found and brought back to currency and purchasing power. The lost son was found and brought back to home, and to service.

There is yet another link between the three phases. It is that of joy; joy in the presence of angels; joy in heaven; and then as though the final joy could not be expressed in the terminology of the eternal spaces, He borrowed the figurative language with which every home is familiar, "Let us make merry." Jesus thus made God speak in simplest speech that man might more easily believe. The three are unified by joy.

The three are seen to be one if we dwell upon their differences. The first two give us the picture of seeking of the lost things by the one who has lost them. The third gives us the picture of the lost son seeking home again. I love this parable because in it both Arminians and Calvinists are at home. The Calvinist will lay emphasis upon the first two parts. The sheep made no motion towards home. It had to be found and carried home. The lost piece of silver could not find itself. The woman had to search and find it. The Arminian will lay the emphasis on the third part. The son had to come back before he was received. I am both Arminian and Calvinist, because I live in this parable. There can be no movement back home until God takes the first step towards finding. There can be no getting back home until there is response and return. In the diversities also we have a revelation of the spiritual unity of the teaching.

We are constrained to go further and enquire, Why are there three phases? What did our Lord mean by grouping the three pictures? There is no question whatever in the minds of expositors as to the suggestiveness of the first picture, or of the last. The picture of the shepherd is so evidently the picture of the work of the Lord Himself; and the picture of the father is certainly an unveiling of the heart of God, and His attitude toward returning men. The picture of the woman, on the other hand, presents a phase very often passed over carelessly in modern exposition. Is this second picture a mere repetition of the first? Are the facts which our Lord would emphasize in the second picture a mere repetition of the first? Are the facts which our Lord would emphasize in the second the same as those He would emphasize in the first? Personally I think not. I think there is as distinct and separate a value in the second phase as there is in the first, and as there surely is in the last. One of the most scholarly and devout expositors and theologians in lectures to lay preachers has solemnly warned them against fantastic interpretations, and has cited as fantastic the view that the first phase of this parable deals with the work of the Son, the second with that of the Spirit, and the third with that of the Father. In spite of that warning, I emphatically adopt that as my view, preferring the interpretations of some of the older expositors. Ambrose and Origen held that here, in the mind of the Master, was the thought of the action of the whole Godhead, that of the Trinity in unity. Bengel, Alford, and Stier alike say that in the central picture we have a revelation of the peculiar activity of the Holy Spirit in His business of seeking lost things. Ambrose, Wordsworth, and Olshausen say that in the central picture we have the revelation of the responsibility of the Church in its co-operation for the seeking of lost things. One at least, Oosterzee, has said that at the heart of the parable we have both these ideas, the revelation of the activity and responsibility of the Church in the power and presence of the Holy Spirit. I adopt that view, believing that in this parable we have the unification of the truth of God's attitude toward the lost. For our human seeing and understanding He broke up that activity and revealed the three-fold process. First, that of the Shepherd; His own work specifically. Then that of the Spirit, searching in and through the Church. Finally, that of the Father, welcoming home the prodigal.

Let us look at these first two phases a little more carefully. First, the picture of the Shepherd, or the Son, seeking the lost sheep. We must remember the purpose of the picture—these Pharisees with their criticism and misunderstanding of Jesus, and their condemnation of His attitude. It was in answer to their criticism He was speaking. Why should Jesus have been at such pains to answer the criticism of these men? Not, as I understand it, for their sakes merely, but because He knew that through the age Pharisees and scribes would continue. He knew that to the end, in the midst of organized religion, there would still be the attitude of the Pharisees and scribes, resulting from ignorance of the Word of God, and inability to appreciate the value of sinning men. So keeping the Pharisees and scribes in mind, we can use them as mirrors, in order to discover what God thinks of such attitude whether in them or in us.

When looking at the first phase of the parable, we find a value missing from the second and third phases. It has been said if we accept the parable of the prodigal son as revealing the attitude and activity of God for men, we have to omit a great many things that we have held to be of vast importance in the Christian Church. But we do not admit that the parable of the prodigal son supplies all the facts. It is an unveiling only of one phase. It is not the parable of the prodigal son, as we have already said. It is the parable of the father's heart. In this first picture, I find something missing in the last. In that there are two sons, the younger and the elder. The younger took his portion and squandered it in the far county. The elder stayed at home, and did his duty. Forgetting for the moment the supreme value of that picture, that of the revelation of the Father, look only at the sons. Neither son is perfect. The younger son was a disastrous failure; the elder son was equally a failure in other ways.

So in the third picture we see a perfect father without a perfect son. Going back to the first phase, we find the missing Son; not the younger, not the elder, but the First-born, the Only Begotten, veiling Himself behind the sweet and tender imagery of the shepherd-lover of the lost sheep. We cannot interpret the parable apart from the One Who spoke it. Believing as we do that when He spoke of that shepherd seeking, finding, and rejoicing He was speaking out of His own heart, we find that thus the parable is completed. Here is the true Son Who never took His portion and went to the far country; the Son Who was in such sympathy with the Father that He went after the wanderer to seek and restore him; the first-born Son, the Only-begotten of the Father. That is the first value of the first phase.

Notice the method of the parable, the introductory words. "What man of you?" Jesus was evidently defending His action by appealing to His hearers, putting them in His place, as it were, but on a much lower level. "What man of you, having a hundred sheep, and having lost one of them, doth not leaven the ninety and nine in the wilderness, and go after that which is lost, until he find it? And when he hath found it, he layeth it on his shoulders, rejoicing." What is the motive our Lord suggested? We take this little picture, and the heart is stirred by it. We talk and sing of its compassion. No audience can be unmoved when we sing

> There were ninety and nine that safely lay
> In the shelter of the fold.
> But one was out on the hills away,
> Far off from the gates of gold—
> Away on the mountains wild and bare,
> Away from the tender Shepherd's care.

The spirit of the Christian Church has interpreted the story accurately, but there is no touch or word of compassion as Jesus uttered the parable. He did not say anything about compassion. The motive to which He was appealing in the hearts of these men was not that of compassion. What then was the motive? The value of the lost sheep. This question of Jesus made an entirely commercial suggestion. What man of you, having lost a sheep, would not go and find it, not because of compassion, but because of the value of the sheep?

Thus the Lord rebuked the contempt of these Pharisees for sinning men. There they stood, scribes and Pharisees, with the phylacteries upon brow and around the border of the garment, gathering their robes around them lest they should be contaminated by those sinning men; and criticizing Him for getting so near to them. He said they had no right to hold these men in contempt. If *you* had lost a *sheep*—! But are not these goats? Nothing of the kind. They are sheep. But they might have said, "Surely You do not mean to say that these men are valuable!" That is the supreme thing He did mean. If you have gathered your garments about you lest you should be contaminated by touching some sinning man, imagining him to be of less value than you are, the first content of this parable is this: I am here because these are sheep of My Father's flock. What man of you, on the basis of you commercialism, would not leave the ninety and nine, and go after the one?

Yet there is more in it than that. The method of the Master's figure is that of similarity and disparity. As though He had said, I am here sitting among these men and eating with them, and gathering them familiarly to My heart, first because of their value, and secondly because of My love for them. The value of the sheep and the compassion of the Shepherd constitute the motive of the work of the Son. The Church has caught the last significance, and rightly caught it, and expressed it in hymn and song. Do not let us miss the other.

What then is the teaching of that phase of the parable indirectly? As to the sheep, that they are the property of God, and that all men are valuable to God. Preacher, teacher, worker in the slum area must cancel all such words as "worthless" if they are going to work with this Christ. Do not let us hear any more about these "worthless" people. Do not imagine that sin can make a man worthless to God. *"My sheep."*

As to the Shepherd, what is the revelation? That the sheep is lost to Him, and lost to the flock, and lost to the fullness of His intention. The supreme revelation is that the Shepherd cares, that the Shepherd succeeds, and that the Shepherd rejoices—and I find a touch of tender sarcasm here—rejoices more over one than over the ninety and nine that needed no such seeking.

The direct teaching of the first phase is that of the joy of heaven over the restoration of lost sheep, and the consequent criticism of that attitude that see no value in the lost, the degraded, and the debased. Degraded, utterly so; debased, unquestionably so; but worth leaving heaven to find. It is a long journey over the mountains! It is the fight with the wolf! That is the suggestion of that first phase.

Glance briefly at the second phase, the lost piece of silver. The figure is changed, but the underlying thought remains the same. It has been said that this is unworthy of the sweep of the parable, for the lost piece of silver was of no intrinsic value. Is not that the very point? Was there not fine satire in thus coming down to the lower level; only one piece of silver? Men might say, That is just it, only one little piece of silver, that is about the value of this man. The other nine are the same value each. The nine are not lost. One is lost. Take an upright, dignified Pharisee and put him beside a publican, each worth one piece of silver. That one is of as great value as this one. Here is one great value of the parable to my heart; the value of lost things to God!

Look at the person introduced here—a woman. Stier says, "The Spirit is presented in Scripture from Genesis 1:1-2, and downwards, as feminine and motherly." Scripture recognizes the Motherhood of God. I say that with great reverence, and with profound conviction. We have not read the Bible accurately if we have only found the Fatherhood of God. I take one isolated instance to prove the statement. "As one whom his mother comforteth, so will I comfort you." We have no more right to leave that out of reckoning than:

> Like as father pitieth his children,
> So the Lord pitieth them that fear Him.

Jesus said something that appalls me most for its tenderness, and the marvelous matchlessness of His grace. Standing upon the slopes of the mountain, looking out over the doomed city of Jerusalem that He loved so well, He cursed the city, but how did He do it? Through tears, and with a voice tremulous with emotion in its unveiling of His own attitude. "O Jerusalem, Jerusalem, which killeth the prophets, and stoneth them that are sent unto her! How often would I have gathered thy children together, even as a hen gathereth her chickens under her wings, and ye would not!"

Throughout the Bible this Motherliness of God is presented, and in a most singular way the Spirit of God suggests that side of the unbroken unity of the Divine nature. Or again to quote the words of Stier, "The Spirit is present in Scripture, from Genesis 1:1-2, downward, as feminine and motherly." Yes, but surely there is more here than that. Is not the Church for evermore the bride; and is not that a beautiful phrase that the Free Churches have so largely dropped out of their vocabulary: Mother Church? I will not hand over that phrase to any one section of the church. I am quite willing all should share it, but I claim a part of it—Mother Church. There is suggestiveness in it.

The Church is only Mother Church as she is Spirit-filled. All her motherliness passes away when she is devoid of the presence of the Spirit of God. All the wooing, winsome tenderness of the Church of God is absent when the Spirit of God is absent. Given the whole Catholic Church, or any local church filled with Spirit of God, she is a mother. To show the Divine activity, Mother must be put in the midst, the Motherhood of God.

Again, Stier has said, "It is not the Holy Ghost as He is a hypostasis in the depths of the Godhead, but as He hath built for Himself a house upon earth, and obtained for Himself a possession." The thought of Stier is the picture of the Spirit working through the Church. Here is a woman looking for a lost coin, a coin with an image and superscription. We are always safe in interpreting a figure employed by Jesus in one place by His figure of speech in another. A coin with an image and superscription belongs to the sovereign, the lord of the realm; and a woman is seen searching for that coin.

In Dr. Burton's volume on Luke in the Expositors' Bible he makes a suggestion full of beauty, that the lost piece was one of the ten that constituted the frontlet worn by a woman, which was presented to her in the hour of her marriage. Somehow this piece had become loosened, and she had lost it, and was seeking for it, not merely because of its intrinsic worth, but because of all that is said to her concerning the sacred relationship of marriage. In all likelihood that is the exact and accurate explanation of this phase of the Lord's parable. Thus with matchless grace the Lord revealed the Spirit working through His bride, and what is she doing? Three words tell us, all of them suggestive—lighting, sweeping, seeking. The emphasis here is upon the importance of the quest, not pre-eminently upon the value of the thing lost, nor upon the suffering by which the lost thing can be found, nor even upon the gladness of the heart of God when the lost thing is found. The emphasis is upon the importance of the quest. The rejoicing is the result of the quest.

Silvester Horne took as the motto of his Mission at Whitefields, "No quest, no conquest." Here is the quest. What is the conquest? The finding of the lost piece. When the woman says, "Rejoice with me," she uses the same expression that the shepherd used when he had found the lost sheep. Bengel says that particular Greek word for "rejoice" is used exclusively of the Holy Spirit in Scripture. Wherever that word is used, it is employed by one writing, or speaking in fellowship with the Holy Spirit.

This then is the picture of the Church, doing her work in the fullness of the Spirit. Once again, here are the scribes and Pharisees who are saying, "This is a terrible business. He is eating with publicans and sinners." He says, "No, I am looking for God's lost coin. His image is on it still, though it is in the dust. I am doing something which is preparing the way for the great ministry of God's motherhood through the Church." Then He reaches the heart of it all, and reveals the love of God in the picture of the Father.

The exposition needs application. Where are we? How far have we entered into fellowship with Him in His view of the value of lost things? How far have we ever come into fellowship with Him in His suffering to save them, and His persistent seeking for them, and His joy when they come home again?

CHAPTER 6

THE APPLICATION OF THE PARABLE.
AN APPEAL

Wherefore, my beloved brethren, be ye steadfast, unmoveable, always abounding in the work of the Lord, forasmuch as ye know that your labour is not vain in the Lord (I Corinthians 15:58).

HE apostolic injunction comes with great force in these days of strenuous life, and of need for earnest endeavour. It charges us to forget the things which are behind, and to press forward towards the goal, the completion, the final victory. These words remind us of that perpetual vocation which admits of no vacation, "Wherefore, my beloved brethren, be ye stedfast, unmoveable, always abounding in the work of the Lord, forasmuch as ye know that your labour is not vain in the Lord."

To understand the meaning of that statement, let us see its setting in this letter. It has been objected by some that these words, occurring at this point, seem to be of the nature of an anti-climax, for immediately preceding them is that great and wonderful challenge; "O death, where is thy sting? O grave, where is thy victory? The sting of death is sin; and the power of sin is the law; but thanks be to God, which giveth us the victory through our Lord Jesus Christ." Immediately following that, apparently separated from it, or having but little connection with it, is this sternly practical word of admonition: "Wherefore, my beloved brethren, be ye stedfast, unmoveable, always abounding in the work of the Lord, forasmuch as ye know that your labour is not vain in the Lord." Personally I do not feel that this injunction is of the nature of an anticlimax, even though read in close and immediate connection with the challenge to death. It is when we have come into such close, immediate fellowship with Jesus Christ as to know the triumph of His victory over death that we are prepared for all the pathway of suffering service that stretches before us, and are equipped for the fulfillment of this injunction.

The word "Wherefore" with which the text commences is related not merely to the words immediately preceding it. It is a habit from which we are suffering today of taking a text, looking at it by itself alone, or only in relation to the text immediately preceding it. I enquire upon what argument does that "Wherefore" base the appeal of the text? Not upon the section immediately preceding, but upon a verse in the very first chapter of the letter. In that chapter we have the apostle's introduction of himself, and exhortation to his readers. Eight verses are thus occupied. Then in the ninth verse there is a fundamental affirmation, "God is faithful, through Whom ye were called into the fellowship of His Son Jesus Christ our Lord." "Wherefore," because God is faithful Who has put you into partnership with Jesus Christ, "be ye stedfast, unmoveable, always abounding in the work of the Lord."

All that lies between the fundamental affirmation and the final appeal might be summarized for the purpose of our study in this brief declaration. The apostle teaches that the Church commissioned for work is hindered for the doing of her work by all the things of the carnal life—divisions, lack of discipline, derelictions, and disputes—and he shows that the Church is equipped for the doing for her work by the spiritualities, recognition of the government of the spirit in the Church, obedience to the supreme law of love, and work inspired by the vision of the Lord's victory and resurrection. Having rebuked the carnalities, and revealed the spiritualities, the apostle says, "Wherefore, my beloved brethren, be ye stedfast, unmoveable, always abounding in the work of the Lord."

The text, therefore, is a spacious one indeed, and the only way to come to an understanding of its message is by taking its simplest thoughts and attending to them alone. What is the central word of this text? "Be ye...in the work of the Lord." That is an appeal to the will, the appeal of the writer to the central citadel of human life. The apostle introduced that appeal by an appeal to the intellect, "Wherefore." That is always the word of the intellect. He based his appeal that he will upon their understanding of the fundamental truths with which he had been dealing. He ended by an appeal the emotion, "Forasmuch as ye know that your labour is not vain in the Lord." Like so many apostolic appeals, this is an appeal to the whole life. He approached the central citadel, the will, along the avenue of the intellect, "Wherefore"; and the massive arguments preceding are in mind. He ended by appealing once more to the will through the emotion as he gave one glimpse of the joy, the crown, the glory resulting from service. At the heart of everything is the appeal to the will, "Be ye...in the work of the Lord."

We enquire, then, what is the work of the Lord; for in answering that enquiry, we shall be led to understand what is the work of the Christian Church. The sublimest meaning of this text relies upon its surface. We who bear the name and wear the sign of Christ are charged, not to initiate new movements or discover new methods, or endeavor in any way to help God. We are charged to be "in the work of the Lord." To understand our work, therefore, we must understand His work. I reverently affirm that Christ's work is our work. We shall understand what our work is by understanding what His work is. We cancel the past tense in our references to Him, remembering He is "The same yesterday, today, and forever." If we may see Him at work in the olden days we shall understand His work today, and therefore our work today. I shall attempt to look at His work in the olden days in no other way than by receiving from His own lips explanation thereof in definition and declaration. I propose to cite three instances in which He did most clearly defend or define His work in answer to the criticism of His enemies.

Three occasions come to mind. At the commencement of His public ministry, John records how Jesus passed through Bethesda's porches and healed an impotent man. When they criticized Him for breaking the Sabbath in beneficent work, He answered them in these words, "My Father worketh hitherto, and I work." Later in His ministry he was seen, to the astonishment of those who beheld Him, to go in the lodge with a man who was a sinner, Zacchaeus the publican. When they criticized Him for the action, He answered in those memorable words, "The Son of man came to seek and to save that which was lost." When the scribes and Pharisees murmured against Him because He received and ate with publicans and sinners He answered in our one matchless parable in its three phases of revelation in Luke 15.

They charged Him with breaking the Sabbath when He healed the impotent man, and He replied, "My Father worketh hitherto, and I work," an almost strangely significant declaration. They said to Him, "Thou hast broken Sabbath by healing this man." He said in effect, "God can have no Sabbath in the presence of human limitation and suffering." "My Father worketh hitherto, and I work." The work of God and the work of Christ, continuous and one, was revealed in that sentence to be work born of the Divine discontent in the presence of human suffering and limitation. It is as though He had said to His critics upon that occasion, Sabbath! God can have no Sabbath while men are in this condition. God will forfeit His Sabbath rights in order to make Sabbaths for such men as these. That is the work of the Lord. It is work that sets aside the inalienable, personal rights of God in order to correct and negative and destroy the destructive forces in the world, and bring man back into possession of his lost rights.

To take the second of these words. "The Son of man is come to seek and to save that which is lost." While the first declaration is that He is in union with His Father in work, the second makes a little more clear what that work is. He came to seek and to save that which was lost. There is no need to stay with an exposition of that, but pass at once to the explanatory parable, with which we have already dealt in our previous study. The teaching may be crystallized by saying that the Church is in the work of the Lord in the proportion in which she suffers with the Son, searches diligently with the Spirit, and is able to sing with the Father when the wanderer returns.

How much do we really know of what it is to suffer with the Son for the salvation of the lost? How much have we, who bear the name and sign of our adorable Lord, ever entered into actual fellowship with His sufferings in seeking and saving the lost? It is one thing to sing of suffering; it is quite another to suffer. It is one thing to meditate in the presence of His suffering until the very stigmata appear in the palms of our hands; but it is quite another to know the fellowship of His suffering. How many journeys have we ever taken over the steep and precipitous mountains and through lonely valleys to find one lost sheep? What do we really know of blood and sacrifice in our endeavour to save men? What do we know of the zeal of the house of the Lord which consumes? My own sad but profound conviction is that the Church of God is trifling with her work. I am not uttering censorious criticism. I know how much of sacred sacrifice there is in the lives of individual saints. But take the great Church as a whole; how many know anything of what it is to be in the actual business of seeking and saving men through labour that means pain and weariness, by wounds and suffering? We cannot be in the work of the Lord while we touch the work with dainty, distant fingers. A cheque [check] out of super-abundance is worth nothing until it is accompanied by our own personal sacrificial service.

Suffering with the Son! We are familiar with it; the picture which our painters have painted, and our poets have wrought into songs that we can never sing without feeling the thrill of His passion and the movement of His tender sacrificial love. But let us honestly enquire how much do we know of the perilous journey and the sacrificial service? Being in the work of the Lord means being in partnership with Him in the suffering that is involved in seeking and saving.

We must also know the diligence of the woman who kindled a light, and swept, and sought until she found. I know how difficult it is; how easy it is to say of some case, man in the congregation, youth in the class, some girl or boy in the school; I am out of all patience with them. They are hopeless. Nay, verily! The woman sought until she found! That is the note we need to have impressed upon our hearts, the diligent, persistent search until the victory is won.

To pass to the last phase of the parable. If we are in the work of the Lord, there must not only be suffering with Son, searching with the Spirit, the diligent quest that knows no rest until the lost be found; we must also be able to sing with the Father when the prodigal comes home. I think this last is what the Church least realizes. Can you be merry with

God if the prodigal comes home to you? Would you feel great gladness in your heart if there strayed into your pew a man in rags? That is the test for the Christian Church.

So we come back to the fundamental truth. The foundation for all Christian service is a superabundant conviction of the value to God of every human life. Pause on your way and look straight into the most degraded face you meet, and remember that soul is a dear to God as you are. If we can come to feel this, and know it: if it can become part of our very life; then we shall sing when that soul comes home, and count contact with defilement as a precious thing if it mean that we are helping that one back to purity and to God?

"Be...in the work of the Lord." We can only be in the work of the Lord as we are prepared for the toilsome journey that involves weariness and suffering and conflict. We can only be in the work of the Lord as we catch the spirit of His unwearying patience in seeking for the lost. We can only be in the work of the Lord as His love is so shed abroad in our hearts that we shall in very deed welcome to heart and home and sanctuary the prodigal in rags and defilement, bringing such an one back to the robe, the ring, and the sandals of the Father's house.

Note the words that the apostle used to describe our attitude, or relation to this work, "stedfast, unmoveable, always abounding in the work of the Lord." There is no redundancy of words here. No single one is useless. Each has a different significance. "Stedfast," that suggests settled constancy in work. "Unmoveable" suggests settled constancy as against opposition. That worker for God is the honoured one who is characterized by fidelity. Sometimes I think there are Christians who will never get to heaven unless they die in a revival, for only then are they active! Others I know who are always in their places, Sabbath by Sabbath, with the boys and girls around them in the school. Their work is not noticed in the religious press. On that account they are to be congratulated did they but know it. There is no flourish of trumpets, but quiet, persistent toil. They are "unmoveable" as against all the suggestion of the evil one, as against all the enticements of the world, the flesh, and the devil.

How they tried to move the Lord from His high purpose. How the devil tried with insidious temptation. How His friends tried with mistaken affection. How His Mother tried to persuade Him to go home because He was over-working Himself. There is an affinity closer than that of blood relationship. In the spiritual world those are kin of Christ who do the will of God.

"Always abounding." I translate that *always* literally, and it is *everywhen*. I interpret the Greek word *abounding* by its use in another connection. When Christ fed the multitude, they gathered up that which *remained over*. That is the same Greek word. Our service is to be service in which there is that which *remains over*. There is no room for cynical prudence and foot-rules and balances here. "Always abounding"! That is a vocation which admits of no vacation. Do not misunderstand that. It is necessary, in the interests of work, to have vacation, but we may still fulfill vocation in vacation. "Always abounding." Wherever we come into contact in religious service or in recreative life with lost man or woman, there is our opportunity. "Always abounding."

We conclude as my text ends, "Forasmuch as ye know that your labour is not in vain in the Lord." The sacrificial journey results in the finding of the lost sheep. The diligent search in the house results in the finding of the lost piece of silver. The overwhelming passion of the father's heart wings its way over the far distances, and sings its song in the heart of the prodigal in the day of famine; and he answers it, and finds his way home, and the father is merry. "Your labour is not in vain in the Lord." By which the apostle meant to say that the reward of service is the success of service.

When John wrote his letter to the elect lady he said, "I rejoice greatly that I have found certain of thy children walking in the truth." That was his joy when he wrote to Gaius, and said, "Greater joy have I none than this, to hear of my children walking in the truth." When the great apostle wrote to others, he said, "What is our hope, or joy, or crown of glorying? Are not even ye before our Lord Jesus at His coming? For ye are our glory and joy." Not only in the heaven that lies beyond is there reward for service. Take one long journey over the mountains, a journey that costs something, and get your arms about some lost sheep of the fold, and you will have your reward there and then. Be diligent, and sweep, until there flash from the dust the glitter of the lost piece of silver, and you will have joy, and a reward. Let us drop these figures of speech. Have you ever been the means of saying some word that has brought a soul to Christ? Then you have had your reward. The reward of service is in its success, and the proportion in which the toiling and seeking are answered by the singing is the proportion in which already we are entering into the joy.

Yet the fullness of it all lies beyond. There are some strange things sung in revival meetings. I have heard people sing with a most curious lilt;

Will anyone, then, at the Beautiful Gate
Be waiting and watching for me?

I am not sure that the idea is theologically correct; but in the philosophy of Christian service it is true. If I would lay up reward in heaven, I must do it by toil on earth. I think even in heaven there will be the consciousness of imperfection unless I take with me someone else.

The reward of service, what is it? "Your labour is not in vain." It is our victory that is our reward. It is the sheep put down with the others in the fold that is the reward for the journeying. It is the piece of silver flashing again, perchance, in the frontlet on the bride's forehead that is the reward which makes her heart glad. It is the boy at home that fills the father's heart with merriment.

In the present victory of sacrificial service there is ample reward, yet God in grace has laid up far more wonderful reward. All these things shall be found in the day that has no sunset. Our wealth in heaven will not be the wealth of harps provided, or crowns worn, but of the souls we have led to Christ and to God. "Forasmuch as ye know that your labour is not vain in the Lord."

The way of victory is the way of *labour*. Earth is the only place for that. We shall not end our work when we go to heaven, but we shall end our *labour*. The great word of Revelation, so often misquoted, teaches that "They do cease from their labour, but their words do go out with them." The joy of it, the spaciousness of it! The loved ones who have passed beyond are still serving, but they have ceased from labour. We can only enter into the work of the Lord in this world by labour, by sacrificial toil. He ceased from His labour when He ascended on high, but not from His work. His work is still going forward. It is only by labour here that the great victory of God in the universe is won. "Your labour is not in vain in the Lord."

No man or woman who shares the Christ-life is free from responsibility, or is exempted from this high and holy privilege. God help us to understand our responsibility, our privilege. God help us to be in the work of the Lord, not watching it, not criticizing it, not applauding it, but in it; in our own flesh bearing the weariness, in our own mental consecration persisting patiently in seeking, in our own deepest spirit-life forever ready with the song as the prodigal comes home.

May God in His grace forgive the poverty of the interpretation, and bring us anew face to face with His own thought and purpose, and send us forth as never before, "stedfast, unmoveable, always abounding in the work of the Lord."

WELCOME HOME

DAVID RAVENHILL

The day that you saw me, tormented and torn
Filthy, defeated, addicted to porn
You ran and embraced me, then kissed me for joy
And shouted to all, "It's him, it's my boy"
You gave me the robe, the ring, and the shoes
And all I required you did not refuse
You called for a feast, my thought was for bread
Your unfailing love, raised me from the dead
This lesson I learned while I was apart
I asked from your hand and not for your heart
No longer forsaken, rejected, alone
You cleansed and restored me, and said,
"Welcome home"

Study famines in Bible

AUTHOR'S CONTACT INFORMATION

Website: DavidRavenhill.net

E-mail for speaking invitations only: ravenhills@juno.com.

Additional copies of this book and other
book titles from DESTINY IMAGE are
available at your local bookstore.

Call toll-free: 1-800-722-6774.

Send a request for a catalog to:

Destiny Image® Publishers, Inc.
P.O. Box 310
Shippensburg, PA 17257-0310

*"Speaking to the Purposes of God for This
Generation and for the Generations to Come."*

For a complete list of our titles,
visit us at www.destinyimage.com.